They Can
But They Don't

They Can But They Don't

Helping Students Overcome
Work Inhibition

Jerome H. Bruns, D.A.Ed.

VIKING

VIKING
Published by the Penguin Group
Viking Penguin, a division of Penguin Books USA Inc.,
375 Hudson Street, New York, New York 10014, U.S.A.
Penguin Books Ltd, 27 Wrights Lane,
London W8 5TZ, England
Penguin Books Australia Ltd, Ringwood,
Victoria, Australia
Penguin Books Canada Ltd,
10 Alcorn Avenue, Suite 300,
Toronto, Ontario, Canada M4V 3B2
Penguin Books (N.Z.) Ltd, 182–190 Wairau Road,
Auckland 10, New Zealand

Penguin Books Ltd, Registered Offices:
Harmondsworth, Middlesex, England

First published in 1992 by Viking Penguin,
a division of Penguin Books USA Inc.

10 9 8 7 6 5 4 3 2 1

LIBRARY OF CONGRESS CATALOGING IN PUBLICATION DATA
Bruns, Jerome H.
They can but they don't : helping students overcome
work inhibition / Jerome H. Bruns.
p. cm.
Includes bibliographical references
ISBN 0-670-83889-6
1. Underachievers—United States.   2. Motivation in education.
I. Title.
LC4691.B75   1992
371.92'6—dc20   91-37310

Printed in the United States of America
Set in Century Schoolbook
Designed by Ann Gold

To Barbara,
Eric and Ellen

Preface

As many as 20 percent of American public school students may be work-inhibited—unable to do the work of school. They may have the intellectual capability necessary to understand the concepts their teachers present, they may have well-educated parents who want them to do well, and they may have no learning disabilities. Something is blocking them, however, from succeeding. They cannot stay on task, cannot complete schoolwork, cannot finish their homework on their own.

These students are not at all happy with their situation. They wish they were successful. They want to do well and to please their parents.

Work-inhibited students are found in all communities; privilege affords no barrier. Ask any teacher of America's affluent children: "What is your number-one problem?" The reply is likely to be something like: "Children who don't do their work." Even in the "best" schools, teachers and parents struggle to find the keys to help students who may be intellectually gifted, yet who are incapable of sustaining the effort to be successful.

Over the course of several years, in my work as a school psychologist, I conducted a broad series of studies concerning work inhibition. The impetus for this research came from a number of failed attempts, using traditional approaches, to help teachers and parents make work-inhibited students comply with the demands of school. The teachers and parents of these students felt defeat and frustration; it was not unusual for them to go to war with each other over who was responsible for the child's failures.

It is clear that many of the beliefs educators hold about children who won't do their work are based more upon myth than fact. It also is clear that when teachers and parents begin to understand these students better, their own feelings change from resentment to empathy, and relationships with the students improve.

Despite the high incidence of work inhibition among students today, very little has been published to help both parents and teachers cope successfully with this problem. With the encouragement of parents and associates in the fields of both education and mental health, I have written this book to share the insights and remedies that help work-inhibited students succeed.

This book offers specific, positive techniques to help these students grow to greater self-sufficiency. Although it may be tempting for some to head for the "quick fix," the suggestions offered in the second half of the book are best understood and implemented after having read the first half, which describes the characteristics of work-inhibited students and the probable origins of their work inhibition.

Acknowledgments

A great many people have contributed to my studies and the writing of this book. While it is not possible to name all those who have helped, it is important for me to acknowledge major contributors to my work: Elizabeth Austin, psychologist, who contributed her work regarding early-childhood determinants for academic underachievement; Joan Schnyer, school psychologist, who shared information regarding her studies of the relationship between locus of control and underachievement; Phil Lindsey, counselor, who put into practice the recommendations that are included in Chapter 6; and the approximately forty people who served on a committee to study the characteristics of work-inhibited students.

A number of my professional colleagues studied my work, listened to my ideas, and responded with their suggestions: Alan McFarland, clinical psychologist; Maureen Lesher, school psychologist; John Blaha, professor of psychology; Linda Seligman, professor of education; and Albert Edgemon, professor of education.

Elizabeth Outka and Irene Saunders Goldstein provided the editorial expertise I needed to clarify my ideas. A special sense of gratitude is extended to Gail Ross, attorney and literary agent, whose representation was so essential. And thanks to Lori Lipsky, editor, for her support and help in the final revisions of this manuscript.

My most essential source of support and encouragement came from my family. My daughter, Ellen, was an excellent source of information about the thoughts of students. My son, Eric, proofread and helped copyedit the appendices. A final thank you to my wife, Barbara Bruns, who also shared with me her knowledge of students acquired through years of work as a school counselor, for her ongoing encouragement.

Contents

I.
The Problem

1 / Defining the Problem

Some students have extreme difficulty completing their class and homework assignments. Teachers and parents of such children know how difficult it is to help students who *can*—but *don't*—do their work.

Teachers want to help these kids. They come to their classes of twenty to thirty students prepared to lecture, to engage in dialogue, to inspire students to receive information, and to work through a variety of academic exercises.

In response to this instruction, most students do what is expected and are reasonably able to complete their assignments. Others who do not are given lower grades, are placed in lower-tracked classes, are given lectures about the grave lifetime consequences of a poor academic record, are kept after school and in from recess, are not permitted to participate in extracurricular activities, are not allowed to go on to the next grade unless they go to summer school, and do not experience the approval of their parents and teachers or feel good about a job well done.

Even outstanding teachers have difficulty getting these students to engage in the work of school. One such teacher described her experiences with Jason, a third-grade pupil:

> Jason is never a problem in class or at recess. During oral reading, he enjoys being called on and reads fluently and with meaning. He enjoys games and likes to be called on and he usually has an

appropriate answer or question. His major problem—or maybe it's my problem—is completing assignments.

I always make sure he understands what is required. For example, during math I may go to his desk and ask if he understands the directions. If he says yes, I ask him to do the first problem. While I'm kneeling beside him, he invariably completes the problem correctly. I then give him an encouraging pat and tell him to continue working. I then go about the room seeing to the other students.

After a period of time, I come back to Jason to see how he is progressing. He usually hasn't completed anything beyond the one problem we began with. I ask him why, and he usually just shrugs or says something like "I don't know."

When teachers talk about students like Jason, they rarely share tales of success. Rather, they speak of their frustrations about how hard it is to get these children to complete almost any assignment on time or as directed. They say these students are disorganized and have memory problems, since they are always forgetting.

"I don't know what else to do. I've tried everything." This teacher spoke of how she kept students in from recess when they hadn't completed their work. She went so far as to make special transportation arrangements for some students to stay after school to finish their assignments. But when 5:00 P.M. arrived and one student had not yet begun to work, it was time to throw in the towel. "I gave up," she said. "There was no way I could make him do the work."

The defeat and frustration teachers often feel is minor compared to what many parents experience. Most parents want their children to be successful, and when they receive negative reports from the school they usually take it upon themselves to see that their child improves. When efforts fail, their frustration grows and they begin to blame the child and the teachers. Teachers frequently believe it is the parents who hold the key and that they should do more to help.

In a conference with his son's teachers, the father of a very bright eleven-year-old named Mark described the child as always being agreeable, never disobedient, and as being so engaging that he seemed to be everyone's favorite. By day, this urbane, well-educated man mastered complex problems in a high-tech consulting firm. In the evening, he felt useless and frustrated in helping Mark complete spelling and math assignments.

The tension he felt was obvious as the father recounted how, night after night, he pulled from his reluctant child the day's assignments. Then the two of them went over in detail the homework that was assigned for that day. The boy never seemed angry or resentful—the whole process just took forever. In this family, the mother almost never participated in the homework struggle, since she just got too upset. Her husband, being the calmer of the two, reluctantly accepted the challenge.

Mark was the middle child. He had two sisters. Melanie, fourteen, was three years older than Mark, somewhat rebellious, and a very good student. The father described Melanie as being very independent. She always did her work and almost never requested or accepted help from Mom or Dad. Diane, the youngest at eight, was three years younger than Mark. She was described as being an affectionate, contented child who posed few problems.

Mark was an enigma to his parents. Why, in the absence of almost any other serious problems, did he have such difficulty in completing schoolwork? His parents were devoted and caring. Both Mom and Dad were well-educated. Mark's sisters did well in school. Yet Mark continued to receive very low grades.

The parents accepted their responsibility for helping Mark,

but in spite of their efforts, the problem worsened. They received mixed messages from school personnel. Teachers and counselors recommended—at different times—*close* supervision or *no* supervision. The parents were told counseling would be useful—or would *not* be useful. Furthermore, one psychologist did not believe the problem was important. Mark would grow out of it, he said, and would do his work when he was ready.

But the parents were unwilling to wait. They believed the problem *was* important, and they wanted their son to be successful. Unfortunately the public school system did not have a program to help them.

Perhaps in years past—or even now in some communities—kids like Jason and Mark were just dismissed as being lazy. Educators often decide that the problem is the child's. If he or she wants an education, it's there for the taking. After all, schools don't guarantee success.

That response may seem appropriate to some, but for the parents of Jason and Mark that answer was not good enough. If their child is not successful, most parents want to know why and what can be done about it.

Are these students who don't do their work underachievers? Many of their parents would say so, since they receive low grades. Their teachers may also agree, since these students should be able to perform as well as others, but do not.

Defining Underachievement

Jason and Mark may or may not be considered underachievers—it depends on how underachievement is defined and who is doing the defining. Nevertheless, the underlying theme of all definitions of underachievement is that a discrepancy exists between the actual performance of a student and the student's expected or predicted performance.

What is predicted performance? Beginning early in a child's

school career, parents and teachers measure the student's abilities. If Sally, for instance, is a bright child, she "should be" a good student. There is a "should be" for every kid. These "should be's" are often determined through the administration of intelligence tests, or other tests of academic or intellectual ability. Most often these are referred to as IQ tests, and include such instruments as the Wechsler Intelligence Scale for Children, the Stanford-Binet Intelligence Scale, and the Cognitive Abilities Test. These tests and others yield IQ scores such as 87, 98, 111, or 125.

If a child earns a score of 98, the standard statistical analysis predicts that he or she should be an average performer. On the other hand, if a student scores a 125, the "should be" is quite a bit higher. The 125 student should be a better student than about 92 percent of all others in the nation. The score of 87 represents low or below-average academic aptitude. Through the use of intelligence tests and other measures, attempts are made to estimate individual abilities.

These predictors, or "should be's," are not determined solely through the use of intelligence tests. The best predictor of future performance is past performance. Students who are early or apt readers, have a way with numbers, or receive high scores on achievement tests will likely be tagged as having good ability. Likewise, early reading problems and low scores on achievement tests are often used as an indicator of anticipated weak academic achievement. Other yardsticks used to predict academic growth are the performance of other students and expectations based upon age and the grade in which the child is enrolled.

How do educators determine if a child is an underachiever? The usual method is to compare the student's score on a standardized achievement test to one or more of the predictors. For example, if a student receives below-average scores on a reading test while possessing above-average academic abilities, the student is considered to have a reading problem or to be underachieving in reading. This child would normally be given special reading instruction.

What about Jason and Mark? Do they qualify for special help? Probably not! Both boys have consistently received average-to-above-average scores on achievement tests, and parents and teachers agree that the knowledge and basic academic skills the boys possess are reasonably close to what is expected relative to their age, grade placement, and estimated academic ability. These boys receive low grades because they fail to turn in assignments. What may be surprising to some is that Mark's and Jason's academic skills are as good as they are, considering their limited output.

Defining Work Inhibition

Good school systems consider the varied and special needs of individual students and teach them the skills they need to learn. But there are certain students with whom even good schools generally have not been successful—students who, like Mark and Jason, would not at first glance appear to need special help. The two boys had no difficulty learning to read; they are able and articulate. They *could be* and *should be* successful, but they are not. They *would be* successful, if only they would do their work.

So Jason and Mark do not necessarily have learning problems. Their difficulties lie in the *completion of work*. These two boys face obstacles that keep them from engaging in the work of school. An inhibition exists that prevents them from using their abilities and becoming successful students.

A term is needed that separates this type of underachievement from all others. The problem is an inhibition to complete work. Such students here are referred to as "work-inhibited." Simply stated, work-inhibited students are pupils who, in all or most academic classes over an extended period of time, routinely do *not* complete assigned work that they are able to understand and are able intellectually to complete.

This definition does not include students who have a specific problem in just one discipline—such as those who avoid math at all costs, but are competent in other disciplines. The definition excludes students who have a bad quarter or semester and rebound during the next term. It does not include students who suffer a severe emotional experience and are so distraught that temporarily they cannot concentrate or engage in normal or routine activities. Also excluded are those who just give up due to placement in classes beyond their present skills.

Even though students such as Jason and Mark possess rather high standardized achievement test scores and do not have weak skills or knowledge, because of their work inhibition they are underachievers. This is true because Mark and Jason are not as successful as they "should be" and are not meeting their parents' and teachers' valid expectations of success, since these children are certainly *able* to complete their schoolwork. So in spite of their good skills, Jason and Mark must be identified as needing help to overcome their inhibitions to do their assignments.

If this problem were easily understood or amenable to fast solutions, there would be few work-inhibited students. But the causes of human performance problems are complicated and involve constellations of unknown determinants. To see an example of the complexity of interactions involved in work inhibition, it is useful to consider the case history of Sean.

The Story of Sean

Before enrolling in seventh grade in a suburban Virginia school, Sean had lived in other urban and suburban communities and had attended both public and private schools. His new guidance counselor assigned him to rather advanced classes, since his standardized test scores indicated that his skills in reading, language arts, and math were well above average. One reason Sean's parents had moved to their new home was to enable Sean to attend this particular school, which had an excellent reputation.

The first quarter of Sean's school year was very difficult for him. He received F's in all his courses except physical education, in which he got a D. His parents requested a conference with the academic teachers to determine what had gone wrong and what might be done to help Sean get back on track.

Sean's teachers reported that he failed to complete almost all class and homework assignments. During class he was attentive, at times contributed to the discussion, and frequently demonstrated good knowledge and problem-solving skills. But his grades averaged F because of his failure to submit written work to his teachers.

Twelve-year-old Sean was described at school as a friendly, rather quiet fellow who was never considered a "discipline" problem. He related very well to adults, especially in one-to-one situations. He was not, however, as successful with his peers. In general, he was immature. His sense of humor was typical of a younger child and he tended to act silly and giggle in a childish manner. Although he had one or two companions in school—friends from scouting—most of the students did not seek his company and he was the butt of some mild bullying.

He was very afraid of certain boys. His parents and teachers noted that Sean became so frightened of being picked on that on occasion he cried when describing his worries about being beaten up. But in spite of his concerns, Sean was not severely teased, nor was there any indication that he was ever hurt by any of his classmates.

Sean generally did not do well in sports. Physical education classes were difficult at times, for Sean performed poorly in most competitive games. It was in the locker room that he felt most vulnerable to the aggressive behavior of the other early adolescent boys. In addition, Sean was embarrassed by his physique—more rounded than lean.

Sean's parents were distraught that the school system had not notified them of their son's troubles prior to the end of the first marking period. The parents suggested that the teachers were not living up to their responsibilities and that there might have been something lacking in the instructional methods as well as the curriculum. The teachers agreed with the parents that something needed to be done to help get this boy on track. A comprehensive evaluation was recommended to develop a better understanding of Sean and to plan programs that would help Sean to complete his school assignments.

The parents' view of their son was positive—in most respects, Sean was easy to live with. Their only concern was school. If only Sean could manage to complete his school assignments, they thought, everything would be all right. The parents noted that it was not necessary for their son to be the *best* student. All they were asking was that he use his abilities and do the best that he could.

Sean was the elder of two children. His sister was two years younger. Sean's early history was reported as successful. His early milestones were all reached on an expected schedule, with language and speech especially advanced. Sean experienced few, if any, known serious problems during his early childhood. In fact, Sean was a delight during his preschool years, since in many ways Sean was more mature at that time than most children.

Sean's mother worked as a part-time librarian during those years, and family life was comfortable. The parents were both well-educated and kept abreast of good parenting practices.

The parents reported a successful transition from home to kindergarten, and Sean did rather well until near the end of the first grade. It was then that the parents were first informed of Sean's difficulty engaging in independent work. The teacher reported that Sean would daydream, read a book, play with some object, or do almost anything rather than complete independent work. The parents viewed Sean's response to his assignments as a result of a poorly managed classroom. Their son had begun to read in kindergarten and was academically advanced.

The parents decided that Sean might be more successful elsewhere, so they enrolled him in a recommended local private school. Unfortunately, Sean's problems continued. During the next five years, Sean attended four different schools, both as a result of career changes by the father and in pursuit of a school that would be good for Sean.

The parents tried to help Sean by establishing a regular time for homework to be completed—and by cajoling, badgering, nagging, restricting, and pleading with him. He was often told by his teachers that he had a good mind and that he had the ability to be an excellent student. In spite of Sean's limited output, standardized test scores indicated that many of Sean's academic skills remained well above average. Relative weaknesses existed in spelling and math computation that were average for his age.

At home Sean remained a reasonably pleasant child who tended to respond passively to the problems he encountered regarding schoolwork. His interests included hiking, camping, fishing, and backpacking. He enjoyed reading about military history and adventure stories. He played Dungeons and Dragons and spent hours building model airplanes. Although he would rarely clean his room or help with household chores, he was not reluctant to cook his own food and occasionally helped prepare the family dinner.

From the parents' perspective, the arrival of a second child was not an exceptionally negative experience for Sean. As his sister grew older, Sean would occasionally tease her, but no severe rivalry existed between the two.

Following the meeting with his teachers, a comprehensive evaluation of Sean's educational skills was completed using the Woodcock Reading Mastery Test, Key Math Test, Test of Written Language, and the Wide Range Achievement Test. The results were not surprising to his teachers or his parents. All Sean's reading skills were judged above average to superior. His math computation skills were below average, while his math concepts were average to above average. His thinking for written expression and his language expression were good for his age and grade, and his spelling skills were somewhat weak.

An occupational therapist evaluated Sean's physical and visual perceptual abilities. No substantive weaknesses in visual perceptual, fine-, or gross-motor functioning were found.

A psychological evaluation revealed that, overall, Sean possessed nearly superior intellectual abilities. No higher level cognitive weaknesses were noted. However, Sean performed poorly on tasks that required him to use a pencil or pen to perform copying assignments.

In addition to the evaluation of Sean's intellectual abilities, a psychologist interviewed Sean on several occasions and used a variety of personality tests to determine emotional factors that may have hampered Sean in the development of friends, doing his work, relating to adults, or feeling positive about himself. Sean responded in a guarded manner and denied that he was significantly troubled. He just stated that he disliked homework and found school to be boring.

Sean's responses to the Thematic Apperception Test and the Rorschach revealed that he was indeed concerned over his life situation. He projected significant feelings of inadequacy. He wanted very much to be successful and well-liked, to be someone special, and to please his parents. He was worried about not meeting implied standards. He was angry, but his tolerance for aggression was so low that he was able to express his anger only in a passive style. Not doing homework was interpreted by the psychologist as an angry response—a quiet, passive-aggressive means of engendering the wrath of authority figures, including parents. Low self-confidence also made it difficult for Sean to sustain independent effort.

The response of Sean's educators was resolute. They decided that the best course of action to help Sean was to pull out all the stops and *force* this passive-aggressive twelve-year-old, who lacked academic and social confidence, to do his work. As he would begin to complete his assignments, habits would be built. By the time Sean entered high school, the theory was, he would be on his way to becoming a good student. Sean had good abilities with reasonably good skills, they knew, and he needed help now. If they left him alone, it would soon be too late to help him.

A series of meetings were held where the principal, counselor, school psychologist, and teachers met with the parents. The school staff developed an intricate program of supervision whereby everyone involved would work together to make Sean do his work.

The daily program began each day in Sean's homeroom where the teacher gave Sean an assignment sheet. Sean took this sheet to each class and each teacher signed the sheet if the assigned classwork had been completed. If Sean failed to complete any in-school assignments, he had to remain after school until they were finished.

The sheet also had room to list the day's homework assignments. Each evening Sean took this list home and his parents supervised completion of the assignments. In the morning Sean gave the assignment sheet to his homeroom teacher, who checked to see if the parents had signed the sheet. If Sean forgot the sheet or if it was not signed, he was sent home. His mother would then bring him back to school, assignment sheet in hand.

The gun was thus kept to Sean's head throughout the remainder of seventh grade. Through the demanding efforts of all concerned, Sean's grades improved—from F to D.

Sean quietly fought the system every day. He hated the assignment sheet. He felt humiliated and his anger grew. There was no evidence that his peer relations improved or that he gained in academic knowledge. After the difficult seventh grade, Sean's parents notified the school that they were not going to engage in another year of nightly supervision. The parents sought the advice of others, including three psychologists, learning disability specialists, and other parents.

Sean's parents believed that their son's problems were possibly caused by a subtle learning disability left undetected through previous evaluations. But further evaluations failed to confirm this. Psychotherapy for Sean and his family was recommended to the parents by two of the three psychologists. The parents, however, did not place either Sean or themselves in a treatment program.

This pattern of failure continued through ninth grade. During those two years, Sean's parents frequently voiced their displeasure to teachers, counselors, and the principal. The parents claimed the administration and the teachers were incompetent.

After his freshman year of high school, Sean and his family moved to another city. While no reports are available regarding Sean's performance in his new school, it is likely that his academic performance did not improve dramatically.

While Sean consistently failed to complete the majority of his academic assignments, he nevertheless did well in activities that appealed to him. He regularly worked long hours on the stage crew, and he usually earned average to above-average marks in subjects such as art, music, industrial arts, and computer education. Sean had good relationships with some teachers and as he grew older, he developed more friendships.

It is sad to note the pain that Sean, his parents, and his educators experienced regarding Sean's work inhibition, which interfered with enjoying and appreciating Sean's many fine qualities.

Too often teachers and parents do nothing in the hope that the problem of work inhibition will go away. This was not true in the case of Sean. Parents and educators established a coordinated plan and worked hard to change Sean's work patterns. Unfortunately, these efforts did not yield positive outcomes for Sean, his parents, or his teachers.

The purpose of this book is to offer parents and educators some courses of action that will yield beneficial results—methods that were not tried with Sean. As with other human performance problems, there is no one simple cause or one single response that will make the changes hoped for. If the problem is carefully defined and described, however, these students need not be an enigma, and sensible, considerate courses of action can be developed.

The following chapters provide answers to these questions: What is the extent of the problem? What are the characteristics of work-inhibited students? What are the possible causes of work inhibition? What can be done to help these students grow toward self-sufficiency?

2 / Who Is
Work-Inhibited?

When the author began his studies of work inhibition in 1985, the focus was to discover how many students were work-inhibited and if they shared any common traits. Were these children of below-average intelligence? Did they tend to be the students who caused discipline problems in the classroom? Were many from single-parent households? These were all logical questions to ask, but during the course of these studies, it was revealed that the traits shared by work-inhibited students often defied what a parent or teacher might expect.

The first step was to administer an extensive survey to find out which students suffered from work inhibition. To this end, teachers and counselors reviewed the work history of their students or counselees and prepared lists of all students in grades three through twelve who submitted significantly less work than typical students. To be considered work-inhibited, a student had to possess a history of not completing school assignments in all academic subjects for at least two years. The student's whole record—report cards, notes from parent conferences, plus additional interviews with teachers and parents—were all used to study the children's work pattern (see Appendix A).

The findings surprised parents and teachers alike. A full 18 percent of all students enrolled in grades three through twelve were not meeting teachers' expectations for completion of school assignments. That meant nearly one in five students was moderately to severely work-inhibited—a considerable slice of the pie.

At this point, two very clear patterns emerged: both gender and grade level were significant factors in work inhibition. Seventy-four percent of work-inhibited students were boys, a pattern that held true across the grades from elementary school through high school. And while very few third-grade students were identified as work-inhibited, a dramatic rise occurred in fourth grade, when the percentage of incidence increased threefold. In grades four through six, nearly 15 percent of all students rarely finished their assignments. In seventh grade, the problem increased once again, with nearly 22 percent of students identified as work-inhibited.

These dramatic increases in the fourth and seventh grades reflect the two milestones in school when work expectations change. Beginning in fourth grade, students are expected to spend a considerable portion of the academic day working independently. Up to this grade, assignments are generally brief and, if a student has trouble, help is given on the spot. In the fourth grade, teachers can easily see which students are working on their own and which are looking at the ground, tying their shoes, chewing their pencils—doing anything other than completing their work.

After fourth grade, the amount of schoolwork continues to increase gradually until grade seven, when another large jump occurs. At this point, the student no longer has one or two teachers, but rather four or more. Students are expected to take notes, read in several disciplines, do routine spelling and math assignments, and complete long-term projects demanding individual initiative. So it is not surprising that the problem of work inhibition is more noticeable at grade seven.

Once the population of work-inhibited students was identified, it was possible to study the traits they shared as a group, as well as how they compared with other students. An ex-

haustive search through student records was conducted to answer three main questions:

1. Do work-inhibited students possess below-average intelligence or weak academic skills?
2. Are they generally disruptive in the classroom?
3. Does the family makeup affect work inhibition?

The study answered all three of these questions, with some surprising results.

Intelligence Tests

Schools use intelligence test scores to predict potential for academic success. While the use of intelligence testing has been controversial, the wide-scale use of such instruments as the Wechsler Intelligence Scale, Stanford-Binet Intelligence Scale, and Otis-Lennon Test of Mental Abilities may be justified because they work! Again and again, it has been found that high IQ scores correlate with high achievement in reading, math, and general knowledge.

Almost all of the identified work-inhibited students had average to superior intellectual ability scores. Only one student had a score that fell below the average range, and most had *above*-average intellectual ability scores. The average score for all work-inhibited students was 115, which compared very favorably to the average score of 114 for all students in the school system. Furthermore, 36 percent of all work-inhibited students possessed IQ scores that were in the superior to very superior range.

By and large, *most of the work-inhibited students not only had good cognitive abilities, but had above-average to superior thinking skills* as measured with tests of intellectual ability. Imagine how this information might increase the frustration of parents and teachers!

Academic Skills

It would be reasonable to believe that work-inhibited students possess weak academic skills that either caused work inhibition or that resulted from it. However, a study of work-inhibited students' standardized achievement tests yielded dramatic information.

While there are many acquired academic skills, none are considered more important to public school educators than reading, followed by writing and math. In an attempt to know how well students are learning these basic skills, school systems administer standardized achievement tests. Unlike intelligence tests that measure students' abilities to learn, achievement test results reveal the skills and knowledge that students have already mastered. Through the use of standardized tests, educators not only can gauge how well individual students have learned basic skills, but they can also compare the success of their students with others throughout the nation.

The scores of standardized tests, then, are comparative scores. If a student receives a score in the 65th percentile, it means that he or she scored higher than 65 percent of those in the national sample.

In spite of years of limited effort on their part, work-inhibited students' standardized achievement test scores remained high. Some of these students hadn't done much work for years, yet most of them had above-average reading, language arts, and math scores. In reading, the average score for the group fell at the 70th percentile. The math score fell at the 67th percentile and the language arts score was at the 63rd percentile. (Language arts includes spelling, grammar, and punctuation skills.)

In fact, three out of every four work-inhibited students obtained scores above the 50th percentile. Only 6 percent of the total group received even one score that was significantly below average. Thus, as a group, the basic academic skills of these students were average or above average when compared with other students in their home community and across America.

The intelligence and achievement test scores obtained by the work-inhibited students looked much like those of other students in the high-achieving community in which they lived. While not all of the scores were high, the scores did not suggest that learning the basic skills of reading and math had been greatly curtailed through the many years of not doing class and homework assignments. A cautionary note: Students who continue to be work-inhibited through adolescence are certainly at risk for *not* improving those skills in reading and writing that require practice and perseverance to acquire. The pattern of scores revealed that many of these students were not only bright, but also highly knowledgeable. The findings, then, suggest that work inhibition is *not* due to low intelligence or poor academic skills. It is on record that many of these students are smart—they just don't use their abilities.

These findings were further borne out by analyzing the incidence of work inhibition among two exceptional population groups—the learning disabled and the gifted.* It was found that learning disabilities occurred among work-inhibited students in virtually the same proportion as in the general population. Fourteen percent of all students in the school system evaluated either were or had been enrolled in programs for the learning disabled, compared to a 15 percent enrollment in the programs among students identified as work-inhibited.

---

* While students with learning disabilities have at least normal intellectual abilities, they have marked difficulties in learning to read, to write, and/or to understand mathematical concepts. Gifted students have superior intellectual abilities; the population studied possessed IQs of 130 or above.

Nearly 10 percent of all students were identified as gifted, compared to 8.4 percent of the work-inhibited population.

These comparisons suggest that while they may have academic skill weaknesses, work-inhibited students are no more likely to have obvious cognitive or academic weaknesses than other students. Furthermore, it is also remarkable that the incidence of work inhibition is proportionately the same among all strata of intelligence—the nearly 20 percent of the school population that was found to be work-inhibited was distributed among all levels of academic ability. It may therefore be concluded that *work inhibition is not a function of intelligence or weak academic skills.*

Behavior Patterns

Do work-inhibited students fail to complete their work because they are at war with the system? It certainly seems logical that students who are acting out, who are oppositional, disruptive, and angry, will not be obliging in the completion of their assignments.

What was the likelihood that these students disrupted their classes by yelling out, fighting, or even being unduly argumentative and loud? To what extent did work-inhibited students engage in antisocial behavior?

Again the results were striking. As a group, the work-inhibited students were not disruptive. In comparison with the total school population, work-inhibited students were sent out of their classrooms for being disruptive with nearly the same frequency as the general population.

By searching through the discipline records of both work-inhibited and other students, it was possible to identify which students had been referred to the school's administration for being unruly. Three-quarters of the work-inhibited students had never been referred for any disruptive behavior (see Appendix A). Counselors, teachers, and administrators confirmed that most work-inhibited students presented no bothersome acting out or antisocial behavior. *Thus, the overwhelming majority of work-inhibited students are not considered discipline problems.*

About the Families

Investigators have long linked unfavorable family situations with poor academic performance. Demographic studies have shown clearly that low social class or disadvantaged status is a potent predictor of school failure. Children who experience early intellectual impoverishment, which hinders the development of language and knowledge, have two strikes against them by the time they enter school.

While the students in this study lived in a community considered to be generally well-educated and affluent, not all the families were well off at the time of the study; indeed, some families relied on public assistance. While the students' cumulative school records did not reveal their parents' income level, some related information was available that specified parents' occupations and, in some instances, their level of education.

These records showed that almost all parents of the work-inhibited students were reasonably to very well educated. At least 40 percent of all mothers had attended college and all but two mothers had graduated from high school. Work inhibition clearly exists among students from well-educated families.

Much has been written about the dissolution of the American family. It was possible that the unsettling effects of separation and divorce were related to work inhibition. In an attempt to gauge the significance of family separation, a count was made. In the population of 143 work-inhibited students, less than half lived with both parents. Only 41 percent of all work-inhibited students lived with their mothers and fathers. Another 41 percent lived in single-parent homes and 15 percent lived in blended families. Blended families consisted of couples that may be, for example, a mother and stepfather.

Information about the total student body revealed that dissolution of the traditional family is not uncommon. Among all students, it was estimated that 59 percent lived with both parents, 28 percent lived in single-parent homes, and 13 percent lived in blended families.

The number of work-inhibited students living in single-parent homes was almost 50 percent greater than the general population. While this finding is hardly conclusive, the effect of family life on school success obviously must be considered. Later chapters will explore the parent-child relationship as a possible cause of work inhibition.

Research on birth order shows a tendency for first-born children to be more academically able and successful than their younger siblings. How does this relate to work inhibition?

The order of birth was obtained for 141 of the 143 work-inhibited students. Thirty-three were found to be only children and thirty-eight were the oldest. Twenty-six were middle children and forty-four were the youngest. In the population of youngest children, twenty-four were the second in a two-child family. Only twenty-six students had three or more siblings.

This group of work-inhibited students was quite evenly divided in terms of birth order. As many children were oldest or only children as they were middle or youngest. While no formal comparison with the total population was made, it appears that *birth order has little or no bearing on work inhibition*. Thus, while the education and economic status of the parents and the birth order of the child did not appear to be linked to work inhibition, a student from a single-parent household *was* more likely to be work-inhibited.

Summary

Whatever the cause of work inhibition, it is apparent from these studies that it is not related to general academic ability or even to the development of the basic academic skills of reading or math. Work-inhibited students are on a par with other students in terms of intelligence and knowledge, and they exist at all levels of academic ability and skills. There are work-inhibited gifted and work-inhibited learning-disabled students, but they are no more likely to be work-inhibited just because they are gifted or learning-disabled.

The fact that so many students in this particular study were found to be work-inhibited is also of interest, since these students were afforded excellent educational services (see Appendix A) and the children were generally encouraged to do well by their parents. It is obvious that high socioeconomic status does not insulate children from this particular type of academic failure.

There are even more variables to consider, of course. To what extent is work inhibition a consequence of mental health problems? Are work-inhibited students sad, depressed, anxious, or angry? What ties are there between this particular type of school performance and family relationships?

So what traits *do* work-inhibited students share? And what are the causes of this frustrating brand of underachievement? These are the questions that will be considered in the next chapters.

3 / Characteristics of Work-Inhibited Students

I f you want to know what children are like, ask the experts—their parents and teachers.

In an effort to develop a descriptive profile of work-inhibited students, parents and teachers were invited to participate in a 1985 study conducted by the author. There was no difficulty obtaining volunteers for this project. A task force of thirty-nine interested parents, teachers, and counselors was formed.

The study's aim was to describe the behaviors and characteristics of students who routinely did not complete assigned work. The members of the task force were divided into seven groups, each group comprising parents and educators of both elementary and secondary school students. These groups developed lists describing characteristics of students who did not do their assigned work. The initial lists were presented to the entire thirty-nine members; tabulations revealed that similar behaviors were recorded in each of the seven groups.

During a five-month period, the task force met seven times. The group considered the many viewpoints of its members and discussed a variety of studies conducted by the author in the Falls Church, Virginia, school system.

Four themes recurred throughout the research. Work-inhibited students showed dependency, low self-esteem, negative attitudes toward school, and passive-aggressive behaviors. In addition, personality tests given to work-inhibited students and their high-achieving peers revealed that work-inhibited students were guilt-ridden about their poor performance, more sensitive to criticism, and more fearful and apprehensive. On the positive side, in most other respects work-inhibited students compared favorably with their peers. And in spite of their difficulties, work-inhibited students were only occasionally determined to have severe emotional problems.

By knowing what work-inhibited students are like, it becomes possible to hypothesize why the problem exists.

Dependency

A fundamental fact about work-inhibited students is that they *will* do their work if their teacher is standing or sitting right next to them. Under these circumstances, even chronically work-inhibited students will do their academic assignments.

Teacher after teacher recounted similar experiences at all grade levels. One fourth-grade teacher gave up her daily break to supervise one of her students during recess. Although Philip liked playing with the other students and clearly enjoyed recess, he was kept in almost daily because he failed to complete his morning class assignments.

The teacher was repeatedly amazed, however, at how well Philip worked when they were alone and next to each other; Philip finished each assignment with little struggle.

But on occasions when his teacher was not able to remain in the classroom with him during recess, Philip did not complete his work. He only finished his assignments when his teacher was right next to him.

Philip's parents tried to get their son to complete homework assignments on his own. They were advised by a psychologist to set aside a certain portion of time each evening for homework. Philip and his parents had a conference and discussed strategies for the completion of homework. They told Philip

that forty-five minutes each evening were to be quiet time—
no distractions. The TV was to be turned off. Philip's room
was nicely outfitted with a proper desk and chair, and a
good lamp.

Each evening just before the forty-five-minute study time,
Philip was to describe to his parents the daily assignments
that needed to be completed. The idea was that if Philip could
describe what he needed to do, the parents would be assured
that their son understood the tasks and would be able to proceed. Of course, if Philip did not understand, his parents would
go over the directions until they were clear. After this beginning, Philip was to proceed to his desk and complete his assignments independently. When he was finished, he would
have until bedtime to do what he wanted.

X The plan seemed so logical! But it didn't work. Philip usually
began the evening by declaring that he didn't have any homework, that either he had completed it all in school or the
teacher hadn't assigned any. After a few weeks Philip's parents
received a call from his teacher, who expressed her disappointment that Philip was still not turning in any homework. The
teacher and parents agreed that the teacher would write out
the assignments and send them home with Philip.

Now the plan had a chance! Philip could not say, "I don't
have any homework." So each night his parents went over the
homework with Philip. Since he almost always had a difficult
time describing what it was he needed to do, his parents took
turns helping Philip understand.

They were advised to be positive—to be good-humored and
not angry. They worked at it. After a while—it seemed like
an eternity—Philip usually acknowledged that he understood
what needed to be accomplished. He went to his room—to his
oak desk, comfortable chair, and his high-intensity study lamp.
There by himself in this ideal setting, he sat—not making a
sound and never completing his work.

After the forty-five minutes were up, Mom or Dad—

depending on whose night it was—checked the work. The agony—the disappointment—the frustration. It was now 8:15 P.M. Philip never had an answer as to why he didn't complete the work. He didn't know. He was confused. He forgot.

The parent of the evening would then usually say, "Let's begin." And Mom or Dad would help Philip with each math problem, each sentence, each spelling word, and each question at the end of each chapter. Philip would work only if Mom or Dad or Grandpa or whoever sat down next to him and helped him complete each segment. On some nights, Dad would say, "That's not so bad! Look, you can do it!" And Philip would nod and smile.

In this case, as in so many others, Philip would work at school with reasonable effectiveness whenever his teacher was with him—literally next to him. The teacher would not necessarily give any instructions, suggestions, or help—but was just there, next to him. At home, Philip would work with Mom or Dad next to him—but with less effectiveness than when his teacher was there.

A little bit more about Philip: At the request of his parents, a school social worker spent most of one school day observing him. She wrote:

Philip presents as a compliant and willing participant in classroom activities. He is a bright youngster, with a good sense of humor, whose knowledge and skills are on or above grade level in all subjects. During my observations, he displayed no acting-out or negative behaviors toward either teachers or peers. He appeared to be well liked by both. He readily followed directions and participated in group discussion.

Philip appears to have only one problem which is the cause of concern to parents and teacher. He does not complete work assigned as independent work.

During one period, Philip was given a packet of work sheets to do. He slowly returned to his desk and worked for approximately two minutes—nothing else was accomplished for the remaining few minutes of the period. After P.E. he returned to his desk to do his assigned work. For 15 minutes he worked on a word puzzle, but did nothing on the sheets that were assigned and required writing. During that time, he set his watch, talked quietly to another student, looked at his unfinished work, folded various papers, put his pencil in and out of his shoe. After 15 minutes his teacher came to his desk. Philip had no hesitation or difficulty in explaining what he was to do. He had several good ideas about what he could do. He orally detailed what he planned to write. As the teacher looked on, he began to write. She smiled, he smiled, she left, he quit.

Work-inhibited students need help to complete work that is easy or hard. In school, work usually requires the student to write, to be persistent. Even if the work is clearly within their capabilities, work-inhibited students will rarely complete assignments if left alone. They will complete work they find enjoyable, however, so certain work-inhibited students may be very successful in art class, computer lab, or reading.

Another example of successful work with supportive proximity involves four students who were faced with failing eighth-grade English. The principal informed their parents that by passing summer-school English, the children would receive credit for the course. A teacher was assigned to teach the four—one teacher to four students. The instructor decided that he wanted the students to write—something they had rarely done during the just-ended school year—and the summer English class became a writing course.

What transpired amazed the principal and parents: the three boys and one girl produced substantial copy. The English teacher reported that not only did these students produce, but their work was often of good quality. The secret, the teacher reported, was the small class. The students completed their work in class with the teacher next to them, giving ample praise and encouragement. The four students passed summer school English with A's or B's. But the next school term, back in the traditional classroom, all four students either failed or received D's in ninth-grade English.

Work-inhibited students of all ages are clearly dependent upon their teacher's presence and/or help. It may not be as obvious during the adolescent years, but teachers report that work-inhibited students are frequently more attention-seeking than others. They not only ask for help, they also seem to need more support and emotional nurturing than others.

Self-Esteem

To feel like someone special, to please your parents and teachers, to be well-liked by your classmates and to fulfill expectations is to feel worthy. What a gift it is to feel capable of accomplishing what is expected. And what sadness it is to feel inferior, to feel incapable or inadequate, to experience shame.

Parents and educators invariably note poor self-esteem as a central characteristic of work-inhibited students. Frequently the behaviors associated with dependency are also associated with poor self-esteem.

Work-inhibited students express their poor self-esteem in many ways. Some are obviously self-conscious. They hold back not only in the completion of assignments, but also in opportunities to take charge in games and discussions. These students are often constricted; they find it difficult to express their feelings and opinions, and seem to want to evaporate or disappear from the classroom. When they do interact, they are often silly and immature. Their classmates may laugh at them. These students often prefer the company of younger children. They are often shy, fragile, and preoccupied with feelings of self-doubt.

Other work-inhibited students express a false bravado. They declare that much of their schoolwork is beneath them: "Why bother with this drivel my teacher asks us to do? Who needs it?" "I can do it when I want to. I just have more important things to do!"

One student who felt this way was Alberto. As early as kindergarten, Alberto was seen as someone special. He was charming and a little mischievous. His excellent analytical skills were clearly apparent. But in his elementary school years, Alberto began to have difficulty with work. In class discussions he always seemed to lead the way; he was reasonably attentive and did well on tests. It was his knowledge and classroom participation that kept him from failing. His many C's and D's were due to the limited number of class and homework assignments that he completed. Alberto had many ideas, stories, and excuses as to why he couldn't do the work that was expected of him.

But because he was so likable and seemed to be wasting so much talent, teachers and counselors tried to help. Alberto usually expressed his appreciation for their interest and declared that he had everything under control. Besides, he said, he would get serious in college.

It was after Alberto failed all his first-year college courses that he began to accept some help. It was not easy for him to come to grips with the pain of his own feelings of inadequacy. Working with a psychotherapist, he became less defensive and less fearful of failure.

In contrast to the work-inhibited, students who do their work not only have a strong desire to succeed; they also have confidence in their abilities to persevere, solve problems, and complete their work. They have an openness that contrasts with Alberto's phony bravado. While these successful students may not all be outgoing, they usually don't appear to be fragile, since they are willing to take risks and are not fearful of failure. They have confidence.

A Study: Self-Esteem

In a study conducted in 1982, the author investigated the relationship between work inhibition and self-esteem. In this study (see Appendix C) a series of tests was given to both work-inhibited and achieving students enrolled in grades six through ten. The test of self-esteem included four subtests that measured perceptions of self as related to family relationships, peer relationships, success in school, and a general sense of self.

The results were not surprising: Work-inhibited students had more negative self-concepts than did students who performed their schoolwork. All measures of self-esteem were significantly lower for the work-inhibited group, while the greatest difference between the two groups was in self-esteem as related to school. In addition, work-inhibited students had comparatively poor self-esteem as it relates to family. The negative thoughts of work-inhibited students toward school included "I often get discouraged in school," and toward family included "I cause trouble for my family" and "I get upset easily at home."

The students in the above study had parents who placed a high value on education. Failing at those endeavors that are most valued by one's parents takes a great emotional toll. It is possible that parents contribute to a lowered sense of self-worth by reminding their work-inhibited children of their frequent failures to do well.

There seems to be little doubt that work-inhibited students have limited faith in their ability to persevere in academic life. But it is also apparent that these students do not believe they are successful in their relationships with their parents. In contrast to students who are able to complete school assignments, work-inhibited students feel significantly less approval from their family.

A Study: Attitudes Toward School

In addition to the test of self-esteem, a test measuring attitudes toward school was given to the two groups. The results clearly indicated that the work-inhibited students had a more negative attitude toward school than other students. Work-inhibited students were more likely to dislike school and to think that teachers were *not* interested in them or didn't want to be helpful. They were more likely to believe that learning activities were boring or irrelevant. Some felt that if they had a choice, maybe they wouldn't go to school at all.

The significantly lower scores received on this test by the work-inhibited students do not mean that students in either group were either all positive or all negative in their perceptions about school life. They mean only that those students who have substantial problems in completing their work feel more negative about school life than do other children.

Passive Aggression:
My Mother Forgot to Pack My Book Bag

Another characteristic of many work-inhibited students— and one that is often misunderstood—is the dimension of passive aggression. Passive-aggressive behaviors are subtle, indirect expressions of anger. Passive-aggressive people cannot openly express angry emotions and deny feelings of resentment and anger. Feelings of anger are often scary to them; therefore, they feel it is better to deny the feelings than to allow them to surface.

The paradox is that the passive-aggressive person *does* express anger, but not openly. Passive-aggressive children are not likely to say no or to refuse to comply with the directions of teachers and parents. Rather than saying no, they are more likely to smile, say yes and then "forget."

Since it is not unusual for a student to forget occasionally

or to become confused, it often takes some time before a teacher of a passive-aggressive child becomes aware that no one could be that forgetful. Conscientious teachers may at first do everything possible to help the child's organization skills. One such teacher described her experiences with Ellen.

> Ellen was about as disorganized and forgetful as any fourth grade child in memory. Her desk was a sight—overflowing with papers, books and who knows what! Ellen was always a reasonably pleasant child and in spite of supposedly highly superior intelligence, she always seemed to forget to take home her daily assignments.

Ellen's teacher wanted to help, so each afternoon she helped Ellen pack her book bag so that all her materials would be organized for that evening's assignments. However, no matter how well that book bag was organized by the teacher, Ellen rarely completed her work. She remained constantly confused and, as the year went by, the teacher became increasingly resentful. In reality, Ellen's forgetfulness was resistant behavior. While she appeared to be confused and helpless, she was also hostile.

Passive-aggressive behaviors are expressed in many ways; being forgetful is just one of the most common. Some kids are verbal lawyers. They argue any point—and often take the opposite point just for the sake of doing so. These children are very good at picking out the exception to almost any rule. Once a teacher spends considerable time explaining complex directions, the verbal lawyer will bring up some highly unlikely, but plausible, exception. After hearing the student's exceptions, the teacher then has to redirect the class before continuing the lesson.

One passive-aggressive child was asked his opinion of his teachers. Tommy barely hesitated before saying he liked them all. He added that it only upset him when his teachers became angry and yelled at him. Tommy was a handsome eighth-grader who could upset a teacher without seeming to do anything wrong.

Tommy was never overtly disruptive—but his behavior was insidious. He always seemed to say innocently exactly the wrong thing at the most inopportune moment. He embarrassed others without ever seeming to be purposely negative. He developed a terrible cough when a guest came to the class to lecture. He would sharpen his pencil just after the teacher had obtained the class's attention, so the directions for administering the test had to wait until he sat down. His repertoire of passive-aggressive behaviors was camouflaged by expressions of innocence and ineptitude. Tommy's teachers often did not understand their own glee as they gave him low grades.

Another powerful weapon in passive-aggressives' battles is withholding. Sometimes such children *will* do what is asked, but it may take forever. One father called his son "Dilly Dally," since the boy always took so much time to get ready or to do any chore.

One mother reported extraordinary difficulty in getting her passive-aggressive daughter ready for school. Every morning war breaks out. The alarm goes off. The child is awakened. Mom tells her daughter to get up and get dressed. She has a nice breakfast ready. Ten minutes later, Mom checks on her darling—no movement. The child is still in bed. Mom yells. She pulls her out of the sack. The daughter says nothing. Mom selects some clothes and tells her to get moving. Mom has to see to others and get herself ready for work. Ten minutes later, little progress. The child is not dressed. Mom screams. The child moves slowly. The battle continues. The child can hardly be moved to brush her teeth, wash her face, eat her breakfast, put on her coat, remember her books, and move toward the door. After an hour, the lines on Mom's face are more deeply etched. This will probably be her most difficult hour of the day. No crisis in her law firm will equal the frustration and the upset that she experiences in getting her eight-year-old off to school.

Sooner or later the persistent tactics of the passive-aggressive child will result in temper tantrums. But it is not the child who has the tantrum—it's the parent or teacher. When this happens, the child is bewildered and does not really understand why the parent or teacher is so angry. The child is also frightened, because it's scary to see an important adult out of control. Furthermore, the angry response confirms for the passive-aggressive child that feelings of anger are dangerous and should be denied or kept under control.

Procrastination or partial responses are powerful weapons. When a passive-aggressive child is asked to complete some task like taking out the trash, the child may remove the trash from the kitchen, but not from the bedrooms and bath.

Dad asks, "Why didn't you take it all out?"

"Oh!" is the reply. "I thought you just meant the garbage under the sink!"

This child will comply with directions, but it always seems to be selective, incomplete. There is always a need for further directions and extra supervision to get any job completed.

Passive-aggressive persons are effective in slyly expressing their anger to others—even though they may do this unconsciously. Such indirect expressions of hostility may alienate even the most well-meaning, caring, and generous individual. It does not take long for a teacher of such a child to stop trying to be helpful. How can you want to help someone whom you can't stand?

Some children are maddeningly passive-aggressive; in others the problem may be less severe. It may seem paradoxical that these passive-aggressive children are often likable and engaging, yet these negative behaviors are not to be denied. The passive-aggressive child wants to please, but angry feelings push up to the surface in maladaptive ways. The child is often unaware of the depth or unable to understand the angry feelings that he or she cannot express in a direct and fruitful manner.

In time, students' passive-aggressive behaviors often result in teachers with angry feelings. Passive-aggressive children are rarely viewed as discipline problems by school authorities, since their hostility toward authority is so indirect. Yet the anger is there.

Relationships with Peers

Work-inhibited students are not necessarily isolated from their peers. Parents and teachers consistently report that most get along reasonably well with their classmates. For some, socialization is their strong point. One parent had his son transferred from one school to another in the mistaken belief that the child's poor grades were due to an overly energetic social life.

Some work-inhibited students do suffer from poor peer relationships. In the primary grades, they often have more difficulty participating in cooperative play and competitive games. There is a tendency for many to play with younger children rather than with their age-mates since they feel more confident and in control when playing with younger children with less-developed physical and intellectual skills. As noted in the self-esteem study above, work-inhibited students received lower scores on the subtest for perceptions of self as they relate to peer relationships.

A disturbing tendency is that some adolescent work-inhibited students narrow their peer relationships to others who also do poorly in school. Groups of work-inhibited students may reinforce mutually held beliefs that school is a negative environment. Teenagers who do poorly in school and with parents may be vulnerable to negative peer influences.

Poor Penmanship

Many work-inhibited students have poor penmanship. Teachers consistently report that when work-inhibited students do turn in written assignments, the results are typically sloppy and often difficult to read. In many respects, this is not surprising. Work-inhibited students have difficulty doing work—and the hardest work in school involves writing. Issues related to penmanship and fine-motor skills are considered in Chapter 5.

Putting It in Perspective

All is not dark and gloomy, since work-inhibited students want to be successful. Just ask work-inhibited children or teenagers what they would like to change about their lives. "I'd get better grades. The problem is I don't do the work. I could, if I wanted to. It's like I get up and tell myself that I'm going to do it today! And then, I don't know. I put it off and then it's too late."

One parent told of how happy her son was when he did finish a lesson. Others have noted that work-inhibited students relished their occasional good performances. These students want to be successful—just as successful as their parents' dreams for them.

And many are successful. It is a rare work-inhibited student who cannot brag about certain accomplishments. Low grades may blind parents' viewpoints. If you ask, "Tell me what your child does well," some responses might be, "Oh, he's a fantastic swimmer!"; "They love him at the gas station!"; "She's a real entrepreneur, has a lawn mowing business!"; "Bill is great around children, a terrific babysitter!"; "Ann won't do a lick of work around the house, but she works twenty hours a week at the computer store. If she weren't so young, they would make her assistant manager!"

Most parents and teachers believe that most work-inhibited students are not severely emotionally disturbed. Rather, they have emotional conflicts. In spite of their burdens, endearing qualities are often clearly evident. But it is important to test these impressions with objective studies.

A Study: Personality Characteristics

The author conducted a study in 1985 (see Appendix D) using a well-known personality questionnaire that compared fourteen different personality traits. The results of the High School Personality Questionnaire, which was administered to both work-inhibited and achieving students, indicated that *most* personality traits common to work-inhibited students are *no different* from those of achieving students, with some exceptions.

It was not surprising that the greatest difference occurred on the measure of persistence, drive, and sense of duty. Achieving students have strong superego strength (an internalized sense of responsibility to self and others) and consistently score high on this subtest. High-achieving students subscribe to parental standards and obligations, whereas work-inhibited students are more likely to be expedient and self-indulgent, and have difficulty in delaying gratification.

As a group, work-inhibited students are guilt-ridden, fearful, apprehensive, and shy. They worry about not receiving the approval of teachers, parents, and peers. They also worry about not being successful. And, in part, they are not successful because they lack the self-discipline to stay on task. They are often too easily distracted by their own anxiety. In comparison, their achieving schoolmates are much more resilient, less fearful, and less needful of the approval of others.

On the positive side, the scores from the personality questionnaire confirm what has been noted by parents and teachers as described in Appendix A. Work-inhibited students have much in common with their high-achieving schoolmates. The scores of the two groups were not significantly different on fully ten of the fourteen subtests. It is fair to say that work-inhibited students are as likely to be warm and friendly, intelligent, and realistic as other students.

It is also fair to infer from the personality questionnaire and from what we already know that work-inhibited students do have serious problems. These students are very insecure. They feel guilty and troubled about their inability to take care of themselves, to do their work, and to live up to their own expectations and those of others. Work-inhibited students are not tough and resilient. Instead, they are weak and unsure of themselves. Rather than taking on the challenge to do well at hard tasks, they look for the easy way out or give up without much struggle. In school they have trouble following all the instructional rules and might well be discipline problems if they were not so guilt-ridden, so easily intimidated and threatened. It is not surprising that passive-aggressive behaviors are common among work-inhibited students, since they are often too afraid to challenge others directly.

Work-inhibited students in general lack the emotional fitness to stay the course when faced with difficult tasks, and are unable to assert themselves. They therefore need far more help than most students—not only in doing their work, but also in developing a sense of adequacy. In Chapter 4 consideration is given to why certain children come to school so lacking in the strength necessary to be independent and successful.

A Profile of the Characteristics of Work-Inhibited Students

Much has been learned about what is and what is not true about work-inhibited students. The following is a summary of the incidence and characteristics of work-inhibited students as presented in the first three chapters of this book.

1. Nearly 20 percent of the school population is work-inhibited; approximately three of every four work-inhibited students are boys.

2. Work inhibition appears across the continuum of students' abilities and skills. The overwhelming majority of such students do *not* have cognitive or central nervous system weaknesses that impair the child's facility to learn.

3. In spite of a history of work inhibition, these students frequently have good academic knowledge and skills. The skills most likely to suffer are math computation, spelling, and written composition.

4. The pattern of difficulty in completing work begins in the primary grades and is frequently obvious by grade four.

5. The earlier the work-inhibited behavior occurs, the more serious it usually becomes and the more difficult it is to change.

6. The overwhelming majority of work-inhibited students want to receive good grades and to be viewed as successful.

7. Work-inhibited students enjoy learning and frequently engage in classroom discussions.

8. Work-inhibited students will complete those tasks that are pleasurable.

9. Work-inhibited students frequently like their teachers.

10. Work-inhibited students have trouble completing schoolwork in all or most classes. These students' difficulties are not tied to one teacher or to a particular dislike of one subject.

11. Although some work-inhibited students may be disrup-

tive, the overwhelming majority do not overtly interfere with the instructional process provided for others.

12. Parents and teachers of work-inhibited students frequently report that the child's only problem seems to be in completing work.

13. These students engage in wishful thinking regarding their work: "Tomorrow I will get organized and get my work done."

14. Work-inhibited students do not usually refuse overtly to complete assignments. In general, they just while away the time and either don't turn in their assignments or else complete the very minimum that will be accepted.

15. Work-inhibited students tend to be dependent upon close supervision and help from others to complete their work and frequently seek their teachers' attention. This is particularly evident in the primary grades.

16. Teachers and parents report that these students are poorly organized. Their rooms and desks are a mess. They frequently lose things. They don't pay attention to details.

17. Work-inhibited students display poor penmanship and generally turn in sloppy-looking and disorganized paperwork.

18. Work-inhibited boys do not often display athletic proficiency.

19. Work-inhibited students have poor academic self-esteem. Other facets of self-esteem may be poor, but are not necessarily so. The greater the value placed by parents on school achievement, the more likely the child's self-esteem will be impaired within the family.

20. Many work-inhibited students have adopted passive-aggressive behaviors, i.e., they react to difficulties by being irritable and indirectly obstructive.

21. Many work-inhibited students become verbal lawyers.

They are able to articulate many reasons why assignments are irrelevant and often identify loopholes in the rules that would exempt them from the requirements.

22. These students tend to have poor tolerance for frustration and give up easily when tasks become difficult.

23. Work-inhibited students often have poor superego strength—they tend to disregard obligations and parental standards. Although most work-inhibited students do not have severe emotional problems, some experience depression, anxiety, and/or anger.

4 / Early Determinants of Work Inhibition

Matthew

"Why is it so difficult for my son to spend just a few hours a week doing homework? I know he isn't stupid!

"This isn't new, but we certainly didn't worry quite so much when he was younger. He started to learn to read before first grade—even before kindergarten. He wasn't even out of diapers when he could read signs—Stop! McDonald's! Such a vocabulary!

"I don't know what went wrong. Maybe it's something *we* did. Maybe we tried too hard. My husband would say, 'Don't worry so much. He's just a kid.'

"Anyway, at our final first-grade conference with Matthew's teacher—I never told this to anyone—I was really looking forward to getting our rave reviews. You can imagine how I felt when we were told that Matthew didn't seem ready for second grade, that he was sort of lost—immature.

"The teacher, Mrs. Kozloski, had a hard time describing her concerns. She knew our son was not lacking in ability or skills. But she said that Matthew seemed 'out of sync,' that he held back, seemed confused. She also suggested that he repeat the first grade, be given more time.

"Well, I was stunned! And I was also mad. Our child comes to school with plenty of ability, with plenty of love. Maybe the school was the problem. Anyway, that's what I thought, that

Matthew would do better after Mrs. Kozloski. Only he didn't. Things only got worse.

"As time went by, the problem became clearly defined. Getting homework done was like pulling teeth. Believe me, I—we—really tried. I was consumed by this, going to school, meeting with teachers, guidance counselors, psychologists.

"There were so many new beginnings. Nothing worked. Most parents look forward to September when their kids go back to school. Not me. Summer was best. I didn't have that daily struggle!

"Oh, God! It's all so stupid. This kid ruining his life at such an early age! And you know what? My husband and I fight more often about this than anything else. So why? Tell me why my kid is so helpless!"

As usual, there are no easy answers to explain human behavior. All the complex factors that make children behave in certain ways will never be simple to identify. Several factors, however, that often lead to work inhibition have been identified. There *are* some answers to the question of "Why my child?"

But first, a discussion of what is *not* at issue. The cause of the problem is *not* related to intelligence. It has been dramatically demonstrated (see Chapter 2) that students who fail to persist in the completion of school tasks as likely as not possess superior intellectual ability and academic skills. By contrast, students who have less ability—who may have significant cognitive weaknesses and/or specific weaknesses in reading or math—are often able to persist, stay on task, and do their schoolwork.

Nor is work inhibition due to parental neglect. Matthew's parents, for instance, loved him, worried about him, and expended considerable emotional energy on behalf of their son. This pattern has been observed over and over again. Most work-inhibited students come from homes where academic success is stressed as an important pursuit and parents are actively involved in "helping."

Work inhibition is *not* caused by severe emotional disturbance. While children who suffer from work inhibition may be emotionally vulnerable, they are generally neither depressed nor considered severely emotionally disturbed (see Chapter 3).

So what *are* the causes of work inhibition? One way to explore this question is to examine the issue of when the problem begins. Matthew's mother was aware of her son's problem as early as the first grade. Her description was similar to that of many other parents. The first manifestations were observed in the primary grades, but the problem did not become obvious until later. Students do not suddenly become work-inhibited. The problem appears to grow in severity as the child moves from the lower grades into third and fourth grade and then may be felt as catastrophic in high school.

It is rare for a student to *become* work-inhibited *after* elementary school. Fourth-grade students who have a positive record for staying on task, for persistence, and for completing school assignments independently are overwhelmingly likely to remain just as effective in junior and senior high school.

When parents of work-inhibited students were asked to look back at their child's difficulty in completing schoolwork and determine when the problem began, nearly half reported, "Oh, he's always been that way." Again and again parents said that they observed the characteristics of work inhibition before their child entered kindergarten. Typical comments about their children's early years were that they were lovable and affectionate, but also clingy, overly sensitive, and needed help to do almost anything (see Appendix E). Almost all parents reported that the evidence was clearly apparent by the fourth grade.

Kindergarten and first-grade teachers were quick to agree that they can identify children at risk for work inhibition. Eight kindergarten and first-grade teachers were interviewed.

While none assigned much homework, they were all certain that they could identify which of their five- and six-year-old students were likely to be work-inhibited in fourth grade (see Appendix E).

One veteran teacher of kindergarten children spoke for herself and the others:

> In each class it becomes apparent very early on that some children are at sea—they have difficulty engaging in their new social and work life. Of course, they are not all alike. Yet there are some common or typical behaviors.
>
> First of all, they are unable to follow directions. They may seem confused, as if they are in their own world. In any case, it seems necessary to constantly redirect these children, to tell them again and again, to take them by the hand to get them started. Once they are on task, they are easily distracted by other children or even by objects on their desk. Of course, they can do the work. But they don't. And on the rare occasions when they do, they are apt to be imprecise and careless.
>
> These children are generally well-behaved. They don't hit or act out. In fact, they are more likely to be passive and helpless. They love to be helped by my aide or myself. The only problem they cause is that they require so much extra attention. They like to visit my desk. They wander about the room while others are attuned to some task or are at play.

If the characteristics of work inhibition appear so early, it suggests that students begin school already vulnerable to work inhibition. Though they may enter school with no apparent problems, possessing good vocabularies and no obvious handicaps, they may have subtle and significant weaknesses nevertheless.

The key is that these children are not self-sufficient. This insufficiency is likely to appear as early as preschool. When the child needs to be self-reliant—to stand apart, to be resourceful, to stay on task—these abilities and strengths are lacking.

Matthew's basic story is repeated again and again by other parents of work-inhibited students. In the early years, their children remained on schedule in meeting major developmental milestones. Yet the parents knew their children lacked confidence. These children may have done well at home—while they were close to their parents. But they were not successful on their own. In response, parents wanted to help.

Matthew's mother relates, "Believe me, I—we—really tried. I was consumed by this." It seems as though, in each case, parents describe themselves as being involved—perhaps overly involved, enmeshed in helping and directing their children. Since the worry may be immense, it is not surprising that parents do everything in their power to make their children do their work. But despite often superhuman parental efforts, they don't achieve their aim. Indeed, it seems that the more parents try to help—the more they *force* their children to do schoolwork—the greater the problem.

And here is the worst part of all. Parents begin to feel helpless, frustrated, and angry. "I feel like he's wasting his talents, throwing away his opportunities. I'm mad as hell!"

Certainly many parents of work-inhibited students share loving relationships with their children. But these parents often report discord and estrangement in their relationships with their children over issues of work or performance.

What may begin as a subtle problem—something parents hope the child will "grow out of"—often becomes a monster. Early in the child's school life, the problem may not appear serious because the child is clearly learning. Furthermore, the child is rarely a "behavior problem," so early interventions are unlikely. But then, as the reports of failure increase, educators and parents respond with disapproval and, to a degree, with withdrawal of affection, thus ensuring that the child's confidence and growth toward self-sufficiency will be impaired.

Growth Toward Autonomy

Some children come to school secure and ready to be on their own. Others do not. Why do some children have the social and emotional adaptive skills to engage in independent schoolwork while these skills are lacking in others?

At the earliest stages of human development, babies are highly dependent upon adults for food, warmth, attention, and affection. Yet very early, infants display an amazing interest in their world. They are attracted to novel situations and appear to derive satisfaction from exploring new aspects of their environment. So while babies are clearly attached to their parents, they also begin to be autonomous and to master their environment.

One of life's major struggles is the quest for independence. Growth toward autonomy becomes particularly evident in the second year of a child's life. The child is motivated to explore, understand, and control its world. The two-year-old's desire to do things in his or her own way is easily remembered by parents: this period is often referred to as the "terrible twos."

The success a young child experiences in becoming psychologically separate from his or her parents is very important to the child's future. A person who has been successful in separating psychologically from parents is equipped to function independently in both play and work.

With work-inhibited students, a breakdown in the independence process appears evident. Something has gone awry to keep these children from developing the social and emotional skills necessary to function well apart from their parents or other significant adults. Perhaps there is something in a child's unique makeup that makes it difficult for him or her to be independent. Perhaps some children receive tacit messages from Mom and Dad that separation from them is not safe— that they won't do well on their own.

Work-inhibited students have not developed the *emotional*

skills necessary to do independent schoolwork, which often requires children to be on their own, apart from others, doing a task that is neither easy nor pleasurable. Students may comfortably do this work if an adult is next to them, offering emotional support. However, work-inhibited students are not emotionally able to persist on their own.

Over time, children who are not autonomous do not develop a healthy sense of self-esteem. It stands to reason that if they are so uncomfortable doing what is expected of them on their own, how can they possibly feel good about themselves?

The problem evolves into a vicious cycle. As they experience failure to initiate independence successfully, children do not receive the positive reinforcement of a job well done that will, in turn, provide them with the encouragement and good emotional feedback to continue going forth with new tasks.

What children need first and foremost from their parents is a sense of security, of well-being. Children need to be given affection and to experience safety. But love, affection, and safety are not enough. Children also need independence.

As they venture forth from parents to explore their own worlds, children must make their *own* discoveries. Parents need to set the stage so their children can go off safely on their own. An excellent environment for two-year-olds, for example, is a home where sharp, dangerous objects have been removed. A child may be free to find the pots and pans in the lower cupboard. He or she may pull out each pan, explore the living room and the hallways while banging the pots.

Parents can foster their offspring's independence and growth toward self-sufficiency by delighting in their adventures. Successful children know that it is okay to be on their own; their parents support and encourage their independence.

During the first few years of life, enduring personality characteristics are established. While some aspects of personality development are influenced by genetic factors, others are influenced by the environment. It is not surprising that studies in developmental psychology clearly reveal that the first years of life are critical in a child's growth toward social competence. In a work-inhibited child, as with other children, certain attributes of his or her persona often are very well-developed, while others are not. As an example, a third-grader who doesn't do his work may be able to read at the sixth-grade level, do math at the third-grade level, display extremely poor penmanship, and behave socially as a preschooler. Certain aspects of these children's socially adaptive skills are weak. It appears that parents of work-inhibited children are able to nourish bonds of emotional attachment, promote the growth of language and intelligence, and instill a sense of morality. When they begin school, these children appear ready for learning, since they speak well, are often quite intelligent, and they follow the rules. The trouble is that they have *not* learned to be secure and capable apart from their parents. They are emotionally unable to take charge of their social and work responsibilities. In the most severe cases, work-inhibited children may be so inept that any school assignment is overwhelming.

What is it that happens in those years before kindergarten that specifically inhibits or promotes growth to self-sufficiency? Some suggestions follow.

Overprotective Parenting

For the most part, parents of work-inhibited students are neither aloof nor uninterested in their children's activities. Indeed, these parents almost always describe themselves as being highly attentive and involved with their children about almost everything! When this involvement becomes overinvolvement and participation becomes entanglement, problems are likely to arise. The following are examples of overprotective and enmeshed relationships that hinder the development of children's growth to independence and self-sufficiency.

Entanglements between parents and their work-inhibited children are typical when the child tries to be assertive and the parents cannot bear the thought of allowing him or her to fail. Ironically, overprotective parents want so desperately for their children to be safe, independent, and successful that they jeopardize their children's self-sufficiency by not giving them opportunities to manage on their own.

Overprotective parents unwittingly commit many little "sins" that add up to problems later. They may put up physical barriers to their youngster's freedom. Playpens or other harnesses, for instance, may be used frequently to keep their children safe. The root of the problem is worry; fear is always there, compelling these parents to be ever vigilant. They feel the world is unsafe and their child needs to be protected.

Overprotective parents may bombard their young children with messages that reinforce their lack of mastery. Children are told, "Wait for Mommy!" "Watch out!" "Stay close!" "Be careful!" "Don't hurt yourself!" "Take care!" "Wait, let me do that for you." Under a regime of overprotectiveness, young children are kept from exploring and from discovering the world on their own.

The problem that some loving, caring—but overprotective —parents seem to have is a tendency to worry. They try too hard to engineer a safe environment for their child and, in so doing, interfere substantially—with serious consequences. The worries stem partly from a lack of confidence that their children will prosper unless provided with the best of opportunities. There is a need to oversee, to direct, to be involved.

Parents may begin "teaching" their very young children, hoping to give them a "step up" on other three-year-olds. "Why not use flash cards and teach arithmetic to our baby?" these parents may think. "Later on, when our child is in school, I want to be there, right in the classroom, as much as possible." "Every night, we'll make sure our kids keep up with homework, and that it's done properly!"

To some extent it is possible for parents to enhance certain aspects of infant intelligence. Yet the effort may well hinder their child's growth to social competence. Language development, for instance, is particularly dependent upon early experiences. Parents may give considerable time delighting in —and actively helping—their children develop superior vocabulary skills, all the while not providing adequate opportunities for their children to gain the self-confidence to be independent learners. In this way, some children may become very bright—and very incompetent.

Tightly entwined and enmeshed relationships between parents and children are not only fueled by worry and anxiety, but also by another quality common among parents. While it is natural for parents to want their children to have advantages that may have been denied them, for some parents this desire is more pronounced. They hope to realize their own successes through their children's accomplishments. "I am not comfortable with my own self," the unconscious reasoning may go. "Therefore, I will help my child to become everything I wanted to be."

Such drives may make parents steer, push, and direct their children and, as a result, prevent them from *being themselves*. While most parents have distinct ideas about what they want their children to be like, some parents are apt to be overly involved and excessively demanding. When children do not live up to these artificial expectations, parents are likely to become increasingly vigilant. This style of parenting gives children little opportunity to be on their own, to discover for themselves and to develop a sense of individual mastery.

To make matters worse, when their children are socially incompetent and are poor performers in school, their parents often react with disappointment, frustration, and anger. Children of such parents become increasingly vulnerable, since the message they receive from their parents is that they are not worthwhile as individuals. Children of such parents are likely to be even more emotionally vulnerable than children of parents who are loving and accepting, but who are simply overprotective.

Parents Who Overempower

Loving parents are sometimes oversolicitous. They give in to their children's demands and create an overempowered child. While these parents may be well-intentioned, they try too hard and they worry. They worry not only about the well-being of their children, but also that unless they themselves are very careful, they may not foster loving relationships with their children. Oversolicitous parents are prone to give in consistently to the demands of their children, often after having denied the same requests earlier. Overempowered children are tacitly permitted to be in charge.

All parents know what it's like to give in reluctantly to their children's demands. A scene common in any supermarket on any given day is a preschooler who is begging a parent for a candy bar. Children beg, cry, throw temper tantrums, flatter, and employ countless techniques to get what they want. After saying no repeatedly, many parents just cave in and comply.

Negotiation per se is not bad—children need to have some power. But there is a need for balance. Problems occur when a child becomes overempowered and is permitted (often unconsciously) to run the show. An overempowered child is a spoiled child.

Children do not become spoiled because their parents give them too much love and affection. Rather, a spoiled child is the product of parents who have difficulty saying no and meaning it. Parents who are able to set limits and who do not give in to whining, cajoling, or temper tantrums promote the separation—and independence—necessary for children to acquire mature coping skills.

Some parents of overempowered children *don't* have trouble

saying no. They say no repeatedly—but then give in anyway. Children learn that if they beg, plead, whine, throw a tantrum—just persist in their demands—they will get what they want. Parents of these children have trouble ignoring these behaviors and in being consistently firm when the answer is "no."

Overempowered children characteristically have difficulty being apart from their parents. When they spy their mothers in conversation with someone else—in person or on the phone—they tend to cling and to interrupt. A father may be working for a prolonged period in the garden while his son is nearby and paying scant attention to Dad. But as soon as Dad strikes up a conversation with a neighbor, the son scampers over to his father, attaches himself to his leg, and begins to clamor for attention.

These demanding children know that they have the power to control their parents. While they often get what they want, they pay a price for their victories. Such children are unhappy with their frequent struggles with their parents, and they have additional problems when they are apart from their family. As five-, six-, and seven-year-olds, these overempowered children do not do well with their peers, since they have not learned through family interactions to become appropriately assertive. They lack self-confidence and often choose to play with younger children whom they can dominate. Their lack of confidence may lead to distrust of their own coping skills and a lack of trust in others.

Overempowered children may be sneaky; they may display varying degrees of passive-aggressiveness. They lack the confidence to take on the world, so instead of telling someone they are angry, they get back *indirectly*. With teachers, they may sometimes be manipulative—acting and modeling adult behavior—and then at another time behave in a helpless, infantile manner.

Positive coping skills are learned when parents are able to

establish clear limits—by saying no and meaning it. It is bad business to send children a message that the world is their very own oyster. Parents who are unable to say no, or who have difficulty *not* attending to every whim, or who respond to every activity of their children as though it were of the utmost importance, create an unhealthy psychological environment that inhibits the growth of independence.

Parents who practice effective disciplinary behaviors (who are able to say no with consistency) actively promote their children's growth to self-sufficiency. Beginning in infancy, children are dependent upon their parents to establish limits on their behaviors. These limits enable the child to be safe and to learn appropriate social behaviors.

Children must learn just a few basic rules—being safe, being considerate to others, and being responsible to themselves. Parents who insist quietly that their children adhere to such limits and practices give a giant boost to their children's growth to self-sufficiency.

Children need to know that their parents are *not* always thinking about and paying attention to them. It is important for the child to realize that Mom and Dad have interests of their own, *apart* from those of the child. In this way a child may observe healthy role models and begin to become his or her own person.

Parental Disapproval

As discussed above, in order to grow to emotional self-sufficiency, children need permission to be separate. Parents may give such permission by encouraging their children to discover their world. Children's autonomy may also be promoted through parental acceptance and approval of the child. Affection and approval fuel the growth of confidence. While enmeshed parenting may stunt a child's growth to self-sufficiency, disapproval is an even greater threat to children's well-being. It is not surprising, then, that some parents of work-inhibited children are more disapproving than parents of successful children.

All parent-child relationships (father-son, mother-daughter, father-daughter, and mother-son) are important to the growth of children's sense of confidence. In this culture, mothers take on major responsibility for their children, and often too little emphasis is placed on the role of fathers. Since most work-inhibited students are boys, more emphasis is given here to the relationship between father and son.

Boys can benefit greatly from fun, accepting relationships with their fathers. "My dad thinks I'm funny and likes to play with me." "My dad and I like to work together in the garden." "Dad likes to take me fishing with him." Positive, affiliated, noncompetitive relationships between fathers and sons are a powerful factor in nurturing socially adaptive growth.

The following illustrates one relationship and the unfortunate outcomes of hypercritical efforts to make a child successful. Tim, a third-grader, had difficulty doing schoolwork and also found it hard to make friends. No one really *disliked* Tim, except that his teachers expressed considerable frustration with his performance. At school Tim was often found on the sidelines. He did not do well in competitive games. The one boy he spent a lot of time with had similar troubles.

Tim's parents had greeted the birth of their son with joy and anticipation. They did not recall Tim's first years as being difficult, though Dad reported that Mom seemed often to be in a state of worry and agitation. Mom was always there, holding on.

In some respects, Tim prospered. He spoke early and well. He was an articulate child who delighted in being so grown up. While Mom promoted the growth of her son's language abilities, she may also have inhibited his emotional growth, since she felt ill at ease with his aggressive behaviors. In turn, Dad was critical of Mom for "babying" their son.

As Tim grew older, his father became increasingly involved in parenting. Dad did not believe in allowing time to go by unproductively, so he decided to spend more time teaching his son science, math, and athletics.

Sports were very important to the father, who himself had played football and basketball and had run track in high school. He was more than a little disappointed that his son was not athletic. At first he believed that if he coached him and got him involved in sports, Tim would improve. They tried soccer and T-ball.

But it was embarrassing for Dad. Tim was clearly out of it. He had difficulty hitting the ball off the T and, when he did, he could hardly sustain the run to first base. When his team was in the field, Tim was more likely to be staring off into space than paying attention to the game. Once, in a soccer game, Tim was blowing the fluff off a dandelion as the soccer ball went by his head.

Dad gave up on sports and decided that Tim was going to be an intellectual. A walk in the woods with his son became a lesson in botany. Birthday presents usually involved various learning "games." Dad didn't waste time "just playing" with Tim. And Tim did amass considerable knowledge to go along with his good reading skills.

But at school, Tim was not a success—and Dad was not happy. Conferences between parents and teachers became increasingly painful. Dad was openly critical of Mom and the school; he felt the teachers should be more in touch with how to help Tim. He believed that they should see to it that Tim spent more time practicing math and writing and that Mom should stop making excuses for him.

It was difficult for this father to understand that the relationship he had developed with Tim did *not* help his son become a confident, assertive person. The messages Tim received from his overly concerned parents were that he was *not* okay. Dad was always trying to fix him and to change him. Tim was overwhelmed by Dad's energy. From Mom he got nurturing—but also the message that the world was unsafe and he needed to be near her for support and affection. Tim was confused by these mixed and unsettling messages. He was kept too close to Mom and her fearfulness. He did not gain from his father the supportive, engaging approval that should be given, no matter what, which is necessary to grow to independence.

Many fathers think they should treat their son as they might imagine the legendary football coach Vince Lombardi did the Green Bay Packers: "These boys need to be tough, to learn to gut it out! They need to be taught and told how to do it."

The irony is that if fathers want their sons to be strong, they need to give messages of *encouragement, support, and acceptance*—not disapproval! Boys have a better chance to grow into strong, assertive—indeed, courageous—men if they enjoy positive bonding, affiliated relationships with their fathers. So as fathers play with and enjoy the company of their sons, they will also nurture them to become resilient young men.

Boys and Work Inhibition

In many ways, boys are more vulnerable than girls—especially in relation to school and early academic achievement. Not only are boys more likely to become work-inhibited; they are also more prone to have difficulties learning to read, to be identified as learning-disabled, and to display behavior problems. While most boys are not socially immature, are not considered antisocial, and do not have trouble learning the three R's, studies show that approximately three of every four students who do have these problems are boys. One of the reasons boys appear more likely to have learning problems is that they have less language development than their female counterparts.

But the concern over work inhibition is not language; it is the development of social skills. Not only do girls generally do better with language, reading, and writing; they are also socially more adept. While some girls are work-inhibited, it is far more likely that girls will begin school ready to be successful apart from their parents. In school, only one out of every ten girls is work-inhibited, but three out of every ten boys will have this problem.

Why are there such gender differences? The answer may be in the way boys and girls are taught to gain mastery. Boys are much more likely to be combative than girls. Most young boys enjoy rough-and-tumble play and are not reluctant to use threats, to push, shove, and hit to get what they want. Girls are much less likely to display such aggressive behaviors.

But aggressiveness—or assertiveness—is not all bad. In this culture, establishing dominance is often exalted. It is "good" to be an aggressive go-getter, a heavy hitter. It is praiseworthy to "never give up." "Whatever we do, we do with all our might." "If at first you don't succeed, try, try again." And as long as aggressiveness proceeds according to the rules of the game, it is okay.

Boys—more than girls—feel the need to take on the world. They develop mastery through active, sometimes rambunctious, explorations of their world. How a boy learns to express and master his aggressiveness is important in the growth of his sense of self-worth. Boys need room and opportunity to run, pull, tug, jump, climb, to fall and get up and do it all again. As boys grow older, they readily turn to wrestling and combative play using make-believe weapons of war and violence.

Such symbolic expressions of aggression may frighten some parents—"good little boys don't do that"—and lead them to inhibit their children's aggressive or assertive behavior. Or perhaps some mothers overprotect for fear that their boys will hurt themselves or others. Whatever the reasons, the development of social adaptive skills may be inhibited by parents who are overly controlling of their sons' active, outgoing activities. Essentially boys need to be given clear limits as to what behaviors are not permitted and then be given ample freedom to express themselves through physical play.

Stunting boys' movement and expressions of aggression inhibits their growth toward fruitful independence. Some boys' outgoing play and aggressiveness is so hindered that their physical skills may be impaired. They demonstrate poor coordination, do not do well in physical games, and have weak fine-motor skills. In addition, they may be timid in expressing their anger—they seem always to want to please. Not having the courage to express their outrage at being so kept in check, they may express their anger indirectly—they may be passive-aggressive.

A smothering style of parenting often produces boys who do not learn to become comfortably separate from their parents. They are overly sensitive to threat and are fearful. They are observed as both clingy and obsequious when they are in the company of adults. But they are not *truly* compliant, since they do express their anger indirectly—they fail.

When older work-inhibited boys are referred for psychological assessment to determine the reasons for poor school performance, their parents are often surprised to hear the findings. They are shocked to learn that anger—indeed, rage—can be a part of the personality of their child, who is often so endearing. And they are surprised to learn that boys who lack assertiveness often express their pent-up anger by being ineffectual.

Guilt, shame, and poor self-esteem are part of the emotional baggage of work-inhibited boys. They know very well that they do not meet their parents' standards for achievement, competition, independence, or emotional control. That is a lot of disappointment.

Societal factors are also important. Parents treat sons and daughters differently. Despite the gains of the feminist movement, academic and career achievement is still emphasized in some homes as being more important for boys than for girls.

Some parents may be more demanding, restrictive, or punishing toward sons than daughters. Daughters are more likely to be offered more nurturing and acceptance.

The Attached Child

The personality of the child is another possible determinor of work inhibition. Every child comes into this world with a unique set of innate characteristics. Parents often marvel at how each child's personality is unique.

In reflecting on the early years of her work-inhibited son, one mother described how clingy he was. "Temperamentally Brian was an easy child to mother, so nice to hold. He slept at regular intervals, was not colicky, and was not overly active. Even babies have moods, and Brian's was remarkably pleasant and relaxed.

"Brian was very different from his brother, Scott. Scott couldn't wait to bust out, while even as a three-year-old, Brian was much more comfortable staying close. Sometimes I couldn't seem to shake him loose."

Each child has his or her own personality. No one can know for sure the extent to which personality characteristics are determined through experience and to what extent biological factors determine personality. But it is certain that an interplay between biological and environmental factors exists. The way children respond and adapt to others and to life's events has its roots in their own inherent characteristics. Some infants are intense, while others are more relaxed; some are squirmy and restless, while others are placid.

To some extent, children's temperaments determine the manner in which parents respond to them. Cuddly, affectionate, and quiet children invoke certain responses from their parents, while distractible, rambunctious children may bring forth very different responses.

Parents of work-inhibited children often report that, as infants, their children were not unusually difficult. These children were generally likable. They reached for and held on to their parents, which for two-to-four-year-olds was not viewed as a problem. Indeed it was usually welcomed by the parents. Only as children's needs develop for independent emotional skills does the problem of work inhibition arise.

Beginning at an early age, children need to begin to move to independence. Some children clearly bolt in that direction. But all children need permission to be independent; some need more encouragement than others. It is important for parents to understand how it is possible to help their children to feel both bonded and secure while at the same time encouraging them to take on their world—on their own.

Schools Promote Work Inhibition

With the origins of work inhibition firmly located in early childhood and developed as a product of parent-child relationships, it is not surprising that some students enter kindergarten vulnerable to work inhibition. Those at risk—overly sensitive, poorly assertive children—have not achieved the emotional mastery necessary to be successfully separate from parents. They lack the readiness to respond in a positive way to the complex social and emotional demands of school.

While standard educational practices are not in themselves root causes of work inhibition, these practices usually exacerbate the problem. Vulnerable, sensitive, weakly assertive children have difficulty succeeding in environments that stress competition rather than cooperation, that are more negative than positive, that reject rather than embrace, that fail rather than encourage, and that blame rather than understand. It is indeed regrettable that educators are unwitting partners with parents in locking students into cycles of negativism that prevent them from growing to self-sufficiency.

As educators begin to understand the dynamics of work inhibition, they will have the opportunity to work in concert with parents to solve this bewildering problem. It certainly would be a relief to parents if positive programs of intervention existed, where the problems of work inhibition would be identified early in children's school careers, and parents and teachers joined together to help children before undue harm occurred.

In the next chapter, detailed recommendations are given for identifying and evaluating these troubled students. In the remaining chapters, recommendations are made to help these students grow to self-sufficiency.

II.
The Answers

5 / Identification and Evaluation of Work Inhibition

Work inhibition is rarely diagnosed as the reason for children's inability to do work; its symptoms are often confused with other educational disabilities. Parents can certainly recognize when their children have difficulty settling down and doing their work, but they rarely know what causes the problem. Even teachers who observe these children daily are often perplexed. At times both parents and teachers suspect that a child's failure to do work is caused by a subtle learning disability, attention-deficit disorder, or perhaps a fine-motor coordination weakness that impairs the ability to write and complete assignments. These questions must be answered if a child is to be helped.

A successful system for evaluating work-inhibited students must accomplish two major objectives. First, educators must identify those students who do not engage in the work of school. Second, educators, working with parents and mental health professionals, must devise and implement a plan to ensure that each of these students is individually understood.

This chapter first outlines the various roles that school administrators, counselors, teachers, and others play in dealing with work inhibition. It then offers techniques to identify work-inhibited students and advice for developing an individual diagnosis for each child.

The earlier this form of underachievement is recognized, the sooner a course of action may begin. The longer the condition goes unrecognized, the more difficult it is to reverse.

One note of caution: Work inhibition is extremely difficult to diagnose. Identifying students who don't do their schoolwork may *seem* easy, but the symptomatic behaviors of work inhibition are varied and similar at times to those of other disabilities. Yet only those students who are identified as work-inhibited will benefit from techniques designed to help them. The problems and pitfalls of identifying work-inhibited students are examined in this chapter.

Responsibilities

Educators have an ongoing responsibility to evaluate the students they serve. It is especially important for them to identify all types of underachievers—not only students with skills deficits (such as difficulty in learning to read, write, or do math), but also students with work inhibition.

While specific procedures exist to identify, say, the reading skills of all elementary students, few schools have effective programs to identify children lacking self-sufficiency skills. Identified by low scores, the poor reader receives small-group or individual instruction; but the student unable to work alone is rarely properly identified and continues to suffer from work inhibition.

What is needed first in each school is a clear sense of direction—an articulated goal to identify and help work-inhibited students. Principals are key players and are encouraged to take the lead to ensure that identification procedures are implemented.

PRINCIPALS:
DEFINE THE PROBLEM OF WORK INHIBITION

The first step for principals is to *accept work inhibition as a problem* to be dealt with in their schools. Meetings should be arranged for teachers and counselors (and perhaps principals) to discuss the frustration of instructing students who just sit there and do so little. These discussions are likely to be spirited, since recent studies illustrate the deep concerns of teachers who want to know why Johnny doesn't do his work and what they can do about it. Since teachers are faced with the daily challenge of helping these students, they are likely to be highly supportive of efforts to identify and help these misunderstood students.

Once teachers have agreed that work inhibition is an important problem, principals should work with their staffs to institute procedures for identifying students at risk for continued or future failure.

Now, here's the rub! It is very easy to identify work-inhibited students from grade three or four on—but it is already difficult at that stage to change the students' behavior. Unfortunately it is far more complex to identify such students in kindergarten and first grade, when it would be much easier to stimulate children's confidence and self-sufficiency. By the same token, principals of junior and senior high schools will be able to identify easily students who are failing, but will find it difficult to help them.

It is elementary school principals especially who must set up intervention programs ensuring that work-inhibited students are identified and helped early on. Principals at all levels set the stage for treating the problem of work inhibition. Among the many players they call on for support are guidance counselors, who coordinate student learning evaluation procedures within their schools. What follows are suggestions for counselors to identify work-inhibited students in grades three through six, then junior and senior high school students, and finally back to the more difficult task of identifying the five-to-eight-year-olds in grades kindergarten through two.

GUIDANCE COUNSELORS: IDENTIFY THE
STUDENTS WHO FAIL TO COMPLETE ASSIGNMENTS

It is the job of counselors to get to know students, to counsel with them, and to consult with their parents and teachers about what to do on their behalf. While it may not be possible to know each child intimately, counselors can use the vast amount of information they have at their fingertips to identify those students who have difficulty doing schoolwork.

With the support of their principals, counselors may coordinate the identification of work-inhibited students. The task may be easy to begin by just asking the teachers! Counselors should request that each teacher of academic subjects provide a list of students who often fail to complete assignments independently. By the end of the first nine weeks of school, teachers will know which students are having difficulty. With these lists, counselors may then take the next step to determine if the students listed by teachers have substantial problems completing assignments in all subjects for an extended period of time.

This check or validation may be accomplished in several ways. For example, Emily was among the six students listed by one third-grade teacher. Since it was November, Emily had been with her present teacher less than two months. The counselor checked to see if Emily had had difficulty doing her work the previous year by asking her second-grade teacher and by reviewing her report card from the previous year.

In Emily's case, identification was simple—there was no doubt that she rarely completed assignments on her own. Her second-grade teacher agreed that the problem existed even then. While other children were doing their work, Emily would do almost anything other than her arithmetic or language arts assignment. She would talk to and bother other students, get up and walk around the room, or fiddle with something in her desk—anything but work. Both the second- and third-grade teachers concurred—Emily rarely did the work she was supposed to be doing.

For all students identified by teachers as not completing work, counselors should verify whether the problem is true for several subjects and among various instructors. The critical questions are: Do certain students fail to keep up with their math assignment, and, in addition, do they fail to complete assignments in language arts and social studies? Did Tom and Meredith have similar difficulties last school year?

Junior and senior high counselors may identify work-inhibited students by checking their grades. Grades earned in academic subjects (English, science, math, social science, and humanities) are largely determined by the amount of work that students complete. Students who have a reasonable understanding of the discipline being taught and who complete most of their assignments as directed by their teachers earn A's and B's. Grades of C and below are reserved for students who fail to comprehend and/or do not submit completed assignments.

A study conducted by the author revealed that teachers place great emphasis on the completion of assignments when determining grades (see Appendix F). In this study of all eighth-grade students in one school, it was found that completion of academic work was the most significant determinant for academic grades earned on report cards. Even students with weak skills obtained at least C's if they turned in their assignments, while students with excellent knowledge obtained D's and F's if they did not complete their work.

Teachers do not give low grades to students who "try." But they will fail a brilliant child who doesn't.

After counselors have collected lists of students who have patterns of low grades, additional information must be obtained to determine which students are work-inhibited, and to what degree. In secondary schools this may be accomplished by interviewing students and by reviewing their scores on achievement tests.

When asked, students will usually tell why they got their poor grades. "I don't do the work. It's stupid. My grades would be all right if I did the work."

Imagine a counselor meeting with a ninth-grade student to discuss school life and his or her 1.2 grade point average. The counselor will have available from the student's record considerable information, including intellectual ability and achievement test scores, courses completed and the grades earned, as well as other information about the student's activities and history. With this information and a student interview, the counselor will have the information at hand to determine if the poor grades are due to an inability to understand (weak skills in reasoning, reading, math, etc.), or to an inability to sustain effort needed to complete assignments. Either way, counselors will know if the student is completing assignments.

In grades three or four and up, teachers expect students to engage in sustained, independent, academic work; therefore, it is in this time frame that the problem of work inhibition often becomes obvious. In kindergarten and first grade, however, sustaining independent effort is rarely required. Given this, and the brief school histories available in the earlier years, counselors will find it difficult to identify work inhibition before third grade. Yet if counselors know what questions to ask kindergarten and first-grade teachers, students who are at risk for becoming work-inhibited can be identified.

In the primary grades, teachers put emphasis on language and reading skills. When a child has a terrific vocabulary, seems to be relatively content, and is learning to read on schedule, teachers of such children may not suspect trouble—even though the same child may be dependent, fidgety, and in need of extra attention.

Counselors may promote reliable early identification of work-inhibited students by providing teachers with a list of characteristics of classroom behavior typified by work-inhibited students:

✕ TYPICAL CLASSROOM BEHAVIORS OF WORK-INHIBITED STUDENTS

A WORK-INHIBITED STUDENT . . .

- is unable to finish work independently
- needs close supervision or help from teachers in order to complete work
- is unreliable
- gives up easily when frustrated
- seeks teachers' attention frequently
- is poorly organized
- forgets often, or seems confused
- is socially on the sidelines
- has difficulty engaging in both cooperative and competitive play
- drifts off and daydreams
- is in own world at work time
- submits work that is sloppy and poorly done without attention to detail, if work is submitted at all
- has poor penmanship
- displays frequent fidgeting, pencil sharpening, getting out of seat, going to bathroom

Students who display many of these behaviors—even in kindergarten or first grade—are likely to have difficulty reaching academic self-sufficiency. These descriptions are an effective tool to help counselors and teachers decide which students have trouble engaging in work.

It should always be remembered, however, that with five- and six-year-old children, many problems observed may be transitory. Some children may be overwhelmed by school initially and seem to be lost and confused, but then rebound to become remarkably well adjusted after growing accustomed to their new school life. But for most students who fit the given descriptions, early identification may avoid future failure.

Teachers and Parents: Early Intervention

Teachers need not wait for principals or other school personnel to take action on work inhibition. Parents themselves can and should call the school's attention to the problem. Teachers and parents often play a waiting game, hoping that "next year will be better." Unfortunately, with work inhibition, the waiting game only ensures future problems. Teachers and parents may help by insisting that their schools identify and aid work-inhibited students of every age and grade.

Symptoms That Confuse

In many instances it is quite easy to point out students who are work-inhibited. Third-grader Emily had a history of difficulty completing work, even though she also displayed the abilities and skills that ordinarily enable a child to be an excellent student. For some students, however, the diagnostic picture is more complicated since some of the symptoms of work inhibition are shared with other types of disorders.

It is very common for work-inhibited students to struggle with the physical act of writing. These children often appear to be in agony as they awkwardly and ever-so-tightly grip their writing implements. And it is not only their grip that is tell-tale. Their bodies are often contorted, making it physically difficult for them to write in a coordinated manner. Extended writing projects are usually beyond their capabilities, and what is produced may be illegible and of poor quality.

As teachers observe their students struggle with writing, it is natural for them to think the problem may be physical. And parents who want specific, concrete reasons for why their children are so academically ineffectual may believe that their children's work inhibition is due to neuromuscular weaknesses. After all, wouldn't it be extremely demanding to persist in writing if the task for these children is physically so difficult?

Clumsiness and poor penmanship may be suggestive of *both* physiological weaknesses and work inhibition. Other behaviors, such as difficulty staying on task, inattentiveness, and forgetting, may be symptomatic of an attention-deficit disorder as well as work inhibition. It is also possible for children to be *both* work-inhibited and learning-disabled. Similarly, it is possible for individuals to possess weak skills in reading or math while also being work-inhibited.

In order to help work-inhibited students as much as possible, it is extremely important to rule out any other suspected disorders. Differential diagnosis is therefore necessary to distinguish between work inhibition and other problems.

But before going further in this discussion of individual evaluation of work-inhibited students, here is an important reminder: Work inhibition is *not* caused by physical or intellectual disorders and weaknesses. Children are *not* incapable of persisting in their work because of weak fine-motor control, a reading disorder, or any other disability.

Every single day teachers witness the untiring efforts, the hard work, and the persistence of students who possess mild-to-severe mental and physical disabilities. Teachers also observe students with seemingly no cognitive or physical weaknesses, who nevertheless fail to give sustained, independent effort to complete tasks easily within their capabilities.

INDIVIDUAL EVALUATION

What are the steps to diagnose work inhibition? The first step is to notice that something is amiss in the way the child learns and behaves in school. Questions need to be asked. "I know my child has trouble doing his schoolwork. What is making it difficult for him to do what his teacher wants? Does he have a subtle learning disability, an attention deficit, or some type of physical or neurological problem? Is it possible that some aspect of his personality is causing this problem? Could it be a trait that he inherited? I want to do what is right. I don't want to find out five years from now that he could have been helped if he were just given the right treatment or enrolled in the right program."

Parents need to know which factors are and which are not related to their child's educational problems. It is possible through individual evaluation conducted by educational diagnosticians and psychologists either to confirm or rule out academic skill weaknesses, attention deficits, or neuromuscular impairments that may contribute to a child's difficulties in completing school assignments independently.

EDUCATIONAL ASSESSMENT

The first analysis should focus on students' skills in reading, writing, and math. By the time students complete the first grade, it is fairly easy to assess students' basic academic skills. To find this information during the elementary school years, all concerned parents (or counselors) generally need to do is ask the teachers. Teachers know very well if students are mastering the skills being taught.

As children grow older, they take standardized achievement tests. If teachers report that students are able to read as well or better than their age-mates, or if test scores are near or above the 50th percentile point, it is likely that weak academic skills are not hampering a student's academic growth.

If the information from teachers on grades or standardized

test records is unclear, or if it seems that weaknesses do exist, students should be individually tested. In such cases, reading teachers and educational diagnosticians may be available through the school system to administer tests in reading, writing, and math. By using such tests as the Woodcock-Johnson Achievement Tests, the Key Math Test, the Test of Written Language, the Peabody Individual Achievement Tests, and others, parents and educators will learn if it is the student's knowledge and skills that are weak.

Information from such an educational assessment enables educators to adjust instruction and class assignments to meet a student's instructional needs. If a student needs extra assistance in learning to read, write, or do math, it is the school's responsibility to provide this additional help. While remediation of weak skills, in itself, will not prevent or cure work inhibition, a work-inhibited student is even less likely to grow to academic self-sufficiency when he or she has not been taught properly.

If a student has demonstrated good academic knowledge and skills, the existence of most cognitive weaknesses is essentially ruled out. If a child is learning at grade level, by definition he or she must possess reasonably good intellectual abilities. With this knowledge, a parent or teacher may reasonably say, "Okay, I know cognitive or academic weaknesses are not contributing to the problem. What else should we consider?"

EVALUATION FOR ATTENTION DEFICITS

In almost every classroom in America, there are children who experience difficulty with inattention, impulsiveness, and/or hyperactivity. Are some of these children work-inhibited? Of the work-inhibited students, is it possible that this attention deficit may be related to their difficulty in completing assignments?

If an attention deficit is suspected as the cause of academic and/or social problems, an evaluation should be conducted.

What might be asked of the teacher and parents to determine if an attention deficit exists? The following questions may be helpful:

Does the student . . .

- squirm in his or her seat, fidget with hands, and frequently appear to be restless?
- have difficulty remaining seated when required to do so?
- become easily distracted by extraneous stimuli?
- have difficulty awaiting his or her turn in games or group situations?
- often blurt out answers to questions before they have been completed?
- often have difficulty following through on instructions from others, even when it is not due to oppositional behavior?
- have difficulty sustaining attention in tasks or play?
- often shift from one uncompleted activity to another?
- have difficulty playing quietly?
- often talk excessively?
- often interrupt or intrude on others?
- often not seem to listen to what is being said to him or her?
- often engage in physically dangerous activities without considering the possible consequences?

By reading a few of the above descriptions of attention-deficit disorders, it becomes possible to understand why parents and teachers may think work-inhibited students may have an attention deficit. While students with both attention-deficit disorders and work inhibition are often off-task, work-inhibited students do not present these characteristics when they engage in an activity of their own choosing, are not being asked to work, or are at play. Students with attention-deficit disorders present the symptoms even when they are trying to give a good effort, are engaging in an activity of their own choosing, or while they are at play.

Interviews conducted by school or clinical psychologists with parents and teachers may rule out the existence of an attention-deficit disorder. Experienced teachers know what is usual behavior for the particular age they teach. But if parents report positive answers to most of the previous questions, an attention-deficit disorder, with or without hyperactivity, may be present. And if attention-deficit disorder may be present, additional evaluation is required.

One extremely useful diagnostic technique is classroom observation by psychologists and/or educators familiar with the disorder. This evaluation requires that more than one observation session be conducted and that more than one type of activity be observed. Students should be observed during times when they are instructed to work independently, participate in class discussion, and listen to lectures or orally presented stories.

In addition to interviews and observations, psychologists may also use rating scales completed by parents and teachers. Whenever a child is suspected of having an attention deficit, the use of a variety of assessment techniques is recommended, since determining its existence is often subjective. By contrast, it is easier to confirm an academic skill weakness through the use of standardized achievement tests.

If the existence of an attention deficit is confirmed through careful study, appropriate help must be provided for the child. Such help is likely to include a restructuring of the classroom environment to enable the child to perform more effectively given the attention deficit. In addition, use of stimulant medication may be recommended by a physician.

One problem with assisting work-inhibited students is helping parents and teachers to understand the unique characteristics of this disability. It is hard to accept that a child with no known intellectual, neurological, or physical handicaps—

and who seems relatively happy and well-adjusted—is failing. When such a puzzling situation exists, it may be a relief to find a clear, precise label such as attention-deficit disorder. Furthermore, if help is in the form of a simple pill, why withhold such magic? But while stimulant medication may be useful for an attention-deficit disorder, it will *not* help work inhibition. These medications are helpful in enabling children with attention deficits to sustain their attention and concentration; they will not help work-inhibited children to overcome their inability to put forth effort.

EVALUATION OF
HANDWRITING AND FINE-MOTOR SKILLS

As noted earlier, it is common for work-inhibited students to produce illegible handwriting. It is recommended that children with these characteristics be evaluated for neuromuscular weakness.

Through observation and evaluation, educational diagnosticians and psychologists may find that students with poor penmanship do not always have weak fine-motor skills. They may observe that when work-inhibited students use pencils to copy and draw designs and human figures (as opposed to the letters and numbers associated with schoolwork), their execution of these tasks is age-appropriate. Thus a child's problem with handwriting may have more to do with an emotional response to the task of writing than to a physical/neurological problem.

In especially difficult or puzzling cases, a more specialized evaluation may be conducted by an occupational or physical therapist. Of these closely related professions, an occupational therapist is a better choice to evaluate fine-motor weaknesses.

Occupational therapists work routinely with perceptual-motor and hand difficulties. An occupational therapist evaluates a child's dexterity, response speed, visual-motor control, upper-limb speed and dexterity, reflex action, and sensory integration skills. Such specialized evaluation enables parents and teachers to determine if a child will benefit from occupational therapy, modifications to the instructional program, and/or whether at-home activities may help a child to improve neuro-physical development.

In speaking about work-inhibited students, one occupational therapist remarked, "It seems as though I'm always being asked to help children improve their penmanship! I tested one child just last week. The description from the mother was typical: 'He's the last one to complete his written work. It's always sloppy. He resists, he refuses.'

"As the evaluation progressed, it was clear to me that the poor penmanship was not due to weak visual-motor control or neuromuscular weakness. In fact, in the one-on-one evaluation with me, his penmanship was fine!"

When asked about the work habits of children in occupational therapy, the therapist noted, "There may be many determinants for a student's educational problems. The child may be learning disabled, have sensory-motor integration weaknesses, *and* be work-inhibited. But the learning disabilities and sensory-motor integration weaknesses do not cause the work inhibition. I've worked with mildly handicapped to severely physically impaired children who always seem to do their work, and I've often observed students with severe neuromuscular weaknesses to be avid writers." Neurological weaknesses do not cause work inhibition.

Psychological Evaluation

By asking questions and conducting appropriate evaluations, parents and teachers may determine if their work-inhibited students have weak reading, writing, or math skills; limited attention/concentration skills; or neuromuscular weaknesses. But even after ruling out such problems, parents and teachers may want more information. They may want to know about the complex emotional nature of these students. School and clinical psychologists may offer more information about the intelligence and personality of school-age children than any other professional.

It is common for parents of a work-inhibited child to want desperately to know everything possible about their child's learning strengths and weaknesses. Perhaps most importantly, parents want to know specifically what it is about their children that makes it so difficult for them to be academically self-sufficient.

Consider the Davenports, the parents of a second-grader named Nelson. Mr. and Mrs. Davenport were confused and frustrated about why their son was having such difficulty staying on task and doing his work. They had repeated conferences with Nelson's teachers. Everyone agreed that Nelson seemed normal enough. He certainly was reasonably bright, but he acted so silly sometimes and only attempted to do his work when his teacher was right there beside him.

A neighbor of the Davenports recommended a psychologist who specialized in treatment of children and families and who conducted evaluations. With some confidence in their neighbor's recommendation, the Davenports made an appointment.

During the first session, both Mr. and Mrs. Davenport were interviewed by the psychologist. The psychologist was able to put together a rather detailed picture of their concerns about Nelson. Since the problem related to Nelson's difficulties at school, the psychologist obtained written permission from the Davenports to exchange information with Nelson's teacher. The Davenports were pleased to give this permission, since they knew that Nelson's teacher also wanted to help.

Most people who seek mental health assistance depend on others for referrals of good professionals. When seeking psychological assistance outside of school channels, parents are best served by a psychologist who specializes in work with families as well as problems associated with education.

The psychologist suggested a course of action to the Davenports. The evaluation was to include information obtained from Nelson's parents and teacher. Two sessions were to be scheduled to work with Nelson himself.

The psychologist began his work by assessing Nelson's intellectual abilities and personality characteristics. The studies of Nelson conducted by the psychologist were designed to help the Davenports understand their son as a unique individual.

In many ways, it is impossible for the psychologist to know a child as well as those who live with him or who see him in school every day. Nevertheless, a psychologist has the advantage of studying the behavior and personalities of many children. And this is what the Davenports wanted—an objective analysis of why their son was having so much difficulty being mature and self-sufficient.

In the psychological evaluation, Nelson revealed distinguishing qualities about his perceptions of self, family, peers, and school. Through their work together, the psychologist observed how Nelson approached work and the degree to which he persevered through difficult tasks.

Nelson was brought to the psychologist's office initially by his mother, from whom he had difficulty leaving for the session. He clung to his mother and whined his displeasure in a singsong way. Mrs. Davenport reassured Nelson that she would be there when the session was finished. After a short while, Nelson reluctantly entered the testing room with the psychologist.

Once Nelson left his mother, his behavior changed. He sat appropriately in his chair and accepted explanations for the work that was to begin.

Nelson was engaging, pleasant, and nicely conversant with the psychologist. The first session was devoted to the completion of a test of Nelson's intellectual abilities. While the psychologist expected Nelson to do reasonably well, he was impressed with his superior reasoning skills. Both parents and teachers had reported that Nelson had seemingly good intellectual ability, but the results of the psychologist's testing exceeded previous expectations and revealed "gifted" academic abilities.

Although Nelson was personally pleasant and engaging, the psychologist did not find it easy to work with him. Nelson often tried to give up when tasks became more difficult. His responses were laced with comments such as: "This is going to be hard." "Do I have to do this one?" "I don't know." "How many more do I have to do?" "I need some help." At other times when the tasks were well within his grasp, he made comments such as: "Oh, this is cinchy."

In spite of Nelson's reluctance to persevere, the psychologist was able to encourage him to finish most tasks. But the psychologist was never confident that he had obtained the best possible scores from Nelson. Thus, it was even more amazing that the final scores were so high.

During the second evaluation session, the psychologist learned more by listening and observing as Nelson responded to a variety of projective personality tests and psychological techniques.

Countless personality tests are available to psychologists. They include picture story tests, drawings, incomplete sentences, ink blots, and other unstructured techniques that enable the subject to reveal personality characteristics.

Using the Thematic Apperception Test, a child may be shown a picture of a boy at a table viewing a violin. The psychologist asks the child to make up and tell a story about the picture. The child's response may reveal emotional mood, thoughts, concerns, and other sentiments. Since projective techniques have little structure, they enable subjects to reveal their individuality. Interpretation of projective techniques requires much training, and considerable care must be given in not drawing conclusions from single responses.

While Nelson resisted working through many of the cognitive tasks, he was rather at ease in telling stories in response to pictures, completing drawings of himself and his family, and finishing incomplete sentences such as "I like_____" or "I worry when_____."

The results of the psychological evaluation were generally positive. The good news was that Nelson was very bright, seemed to have no intellectual weaknesses, and clearly was not seriously emotionally disturbed. Furthermore, Nelson desired close relationships with the important people in his life and had a strong desire to be liked.

For an eight-year-old, Nelson appeared in some ways to be very mature. He had an excellent vocabulary and a good fund of general knowledge. More than most children his age, he had an interest in world events and geography. He liked to study maps.

But Nelson portrayed himself as a child with few friends. Two responses to the incomplete-sentence test were particularly telling: "Other kids *don't like me*," and "When the others are playing, *I butt in*."

Nelson's answers about work were also revealing. "When others work, *I just sit there and look at my book*." "When something is hard for me, *I don't do it*."

While Nelson expressed affectionate thoughts about his parents, he was also clearly in conflict with them. It didn't seem to matter what the issue was. Whenever his parents asked him to do something, Nelson resisted. This resistance was usually indirect. He just had to be told "a dozen times" before he did what he was told, and then the job was usually not done as the parents wanted.

A clear theme in Nelson's projective stories was anger. For although Nelson generally was not overtly angry, he was able to express this emotion in response to the personality tests given by the psychologist. His feelings of anger were accomnied by feelings of anxiety and concern. It clearly bothered and frightened Nelson that he experienced these troublesome feelings concerning his parents.

Since Nelson had difficulty accepting his own angry feelings, he also had difficulty in expressing them. During the psychological exam, his stories had angry themes. But in everyday life, his anger was expressed in a passive, indirect manner. Rather than being openly confrontational with his parents, he just quietly—and perhaps unconsciously—refused to comply with their demands.

It was not possible for the psychologist to know why Nelson had such difficulty in expressing his feelings of anger or why he was so clingy and dependent. What was clear, however, was that Nelson—like so many work-inhibited students—had trouble gaining the emotional mastery necessary to break away from his primary caregivers to take on the world assertively.

His relationships with his parents were very demanding. He wanted their attention, their affection, and their approval—all the time. He had difficulty accepting any criticism or scolding, and because he had so much difficulty breaking away, he had trouble mastering the responsibilities and work expected for his age.

Nelson was dissatisfied with himself; he knew he was not a success. His feelings of failure amplified his feelings of anger—which frightened him and continued to promote his passive response.

Nelson wanted to break away, but it wasn't within his power to do so. He was able to earn high scores on the intelligence test, but only with the psychologist's continuing encouragement. Whenever he thought something was difficult, Nelson gave up—unless someone was there to help.

Nelson was by no means a monster. Whenever he felt comfortable, he was very loving and affectionate with his parents. Indeed, it may be that his feelings of frustration and anger were so frightening *because* expressing these emotions might put his loving relationships at risk.

Mr. and Mrs. Davenport accepted and agreed with the results of the psychological evaluation. The information fit their observations and the reports of his teacher. With the insights they gained from the psychological evaluation, the Davenports were ready to work with others to help their son.

It is often difficult for parents to seek psychological assistance. Caring parents do not want to hear that their child has angry feelings, does not like himself, or that he is in conflict with Mom and Dad. It takes courage for parents to permit themselves to be vulnerable and seek psychological help. The process is often painful!

Of course, no two work-inhibited students are alike, but many, like Nelson, are insecure, anxious, and angry in a passive, indirect manner. While it is important that parents and teachers have good insights into the unique personalities of these students, there are possible negative side effects of the evaluations themselves.

Parents are cautioned to obtain only those individual evaluations that are needed. If children are taken from specialist to specialist for examinations, it is easy to enhance a child's feelings that there is something terribly wrong with them—reinforcing their already low self-esteem.

Also, parents should consider using the resources of the school system whenever possible. School psychologists and counselors are often in the best positions to know what is going on with children and to understand the dynamics of their learning problems.

If educators begin by identifying those students who are not engaging in the work of school—and if parents and teachers truly get to know their students individually—parents and teachers will be able to support students' paths to academic success. Systematic evaluation methods must be employed to ensure that work-inhibited students are not overlooked, are not consigned to a school career of educational frustration and failure, are not viewed with anger, and are not given a watered-down education that will be a lifetime albatross.

Suggestions about how to help work-inhibited students once they are identified and evaluated appear in the next three chapters.

6 / What Educators Can Do

What techniques can educators use to help work-inhibited students shed their emotional shackles and apply themselves effectively to their work? The suggestions in this chapter are tailored to fit the special needs of work-inhibited students and complement good educational practices for all children.

Work-inhibited students may be helped in a number of general ways. They benefit from positive relationships with their teachers, they achieve more with supportive help to complete tasks, they benefit when they are actively helped to become independent, and they benefit from opportunities to develop their individual strengths.

Building Nurturing Relationships

In order to grow toward independence, work-inhibited students need friendly, positive, and optimistic relationships with important adults, including teachers. These students are generally weak emotionally and suffer from low self-esteem. It is reassuring and important to them to feel that their teacher is in their corner.

Most people tend to do better work—or at least to enjoy it more—when they work for someone who likes them. But a work-inhibited student is clearly more dependent upon positive relationships than a confident student. This is addressed by William Glasser in his landmark book, *Schools Without Failure*. Glasser stresses that reluctant students engage in the work of school simply because they share a positive relationship with their teacher.

Building a positive relationship with work-inhibited students is not always easy; it takes special effort and planning on the part of the teacher. The relationship may be enhanced by the teacher noticing the student away from work, by attentive listening, by ignoring certain negative behaviors, by giving messages of positive expectations, by conveying acceptance, by giving positive reinforcement, and by being genuine.

In one sense these recommendations are not remarkable, since they are not difficult to understand and they are part of the repertoire of effective teachers. The results they produce in work-inhibited students, however, *may* be remarkable. It is quite dramatic how much students can grow away from dependent ineptitude and toward competence simply by experiencing a teacher's nurturing support.

BEGIN BY SAYING "HELLO"

To begin, notice the student *away from work*. Make a point of greeting the student as often as possible. "Hello, Todd, how are you doing?" "Good morning, Conrad, did you hear about Jenny?" "Hi, Barbara, did you see the ballgame?"

Hearing one's name called out in a friendly manner may be powerful medicine to the downhearted. It is an easy matter to say hello on the playground, in the hall, after recess, in the lunchroom—anytime an exchange can take place, a wave, a nod, a smile. Do this again and again, even if the emotionally needy, work-inhibited student doesn't respond, even if only a grunt is returned, or even if the child makes some silly, immature remark.

A teacher's friendliness may be positively disarming to these students. They usually have long histories of negative self-perceptions and do not expect their teachers to be truly interested in them. In response to their teachers' friendly "hello" —away from the classroom, where teachers are not obligated to take notice of them—the students feel a bit better about their teachers and about themselves. Such friendly, inviting greetings in themselves can improve attitudes toward school and pave the way for further positive dialogue.

BE AN ATTENTIVE, NONJUDGMENTAL LISTENER

The act of really listening is a tremendous compliment—and a powerful tool in binding a relationship. Most teacher-student social exchanges are momentary—just a few words and a smile. But sometimes the opportunity presents itself to be with a student in a situation that has nothing to do with schoolwork. Exploit opportunities to be attentive to remarks about the student's interests.

Give the student an opportunity to discuss those happenings that are important to him or her. Find out about favorite television shows, movies, sports, heroes, teams, boyfriends, girlfriends, dances, jobs, whatever. Some students have unique— and strong—interests. Don't reject the morbid or odd. Just listen to what the student has to say. Don't correct or overinterpret.

Responding in kind to what the student talks about demonstrates interest and acceptance: a sad story, a sad response; a shocking, gruesome story—"How awful! Oh, my!" Reflect or mirror the feelings expressed by the child. In essence, respond in a manner that demonstrates an understanding of feelings as well as the content of what has been expressed. At minimum, listen with full attention or promote continued conversation by saying, "What else?" or "Tell me more" or "No kidding, how about that! I want to know how this ends."

By being attentive through careful listening, teachers convey acceptance. This acceptance does not mean, however, that everything the student says may be approved of by the teacher.

Rather, nonjudgmental listening conveys the teacher's interest, caring, and respect. Reflective listening is a powerful technique to bind relationships.

Students occasionally make silly, ridiculous comments that are not likely to be true. It is not necessary either to agree with these or to point out inaccuracies. Students test teachers by telling them true—or perhaps untrue—information designed to determine how "safe" it is for them to share their feelings with the teacher. It is very important not to reprimand or act parental when a student tells of an idea, plan, or event that may not be comfortable for the teacher to hear.

While a teacher should never give tacit approval to anything that might endanger anyone, other negative information might just be listened to and not responded to. For example, it is not *always* necessary to remind a student that drinking under age is illegal, that it is the parent's duty to discipline their children, that "teachers are just doing what is best for you," that "it's not right to fight," or that "you should be nice to everyone."

Bragging and obviously exaggerated stories do not demand comments such as, "There's no way you could have scored forty points!" or "No one has ever done that!" Nonjudgmental listening builds trust, making it possible for continued sharing of ideas, experiences, and feelings.

EMOTIONAL SUPPORT

Before a work-inhibited child can overcome dependency, he or she needs a great deal of emotional support. In a sense, work-inhibited students have to be more dependent upon their teachers in order to gain the strength needed to grow apart—to have the confidence to work on their own.

While it may be difficult in kindergarten and first grade to identify which students will be work-inhibited, it is usually clear which ones are "out of sync." Children who daydream while others are busy, those who always seem to lag when others are doing chores, and those who seem to work *only* when the teacher is next to them may benefit from being treated as if they were work-inhibited.

Some children may grow out of such insufficiency, but probably not on their own. These five- to seven-year-olds are especially vulnerable and, in order to grow out of their helpless condition, must depend on their teachers for support.

Teachers may enhance their student's sense of security through proximity. Place the child's desk next to the teacher's so that the child can keep the teacher in view. Give these students ample attention—not just as a reward for completion of work or for being good, but also as a message of acceptance and caring.

Caring, supportive attention is helpful at all ages and may be given in innumerable ways. It is important that expressions of caring be genuine. Each teacher has his or her own style— a good-natured pat on the back, a smile, a hug, a kidding repartée, a way of communicating "I'm glad to see you."

Secondary school students benefit from the support of interested teachers who communicate acceptance through friendly, positive encounters. It is counterproductive to be derogatory about hairstyle, clothing, or current countercultural heroes.

Avoid insulting or ridiculing teenagers' efforts to be different. Both the secure and the insecure will adopt dress, social mannerisms, and music that are contrary to their parents' interests. As long as these efforts to be an individual are not self-destructive or harmful to others, be accepting. Teenagers need to have fun in their own way, to be well-liked by their peers, and to feel comfortable with themselves.

It does not help children to push them away or to make negative, demeaning comments. Lectures about shortcomings do not work. If they did, work inhibition would not exist!

Sarcasm is an ugly weapon that can be especially devastating to work-inhibited children who are sensitive to threats.

Imagine a seventh-grade student finally completing a math assignment. The work is turned in. The teacher remarks, "Oh, my gosh! I must be dreaming! Russell did his homework and I never believed in miracles!" or "Hey, Russell! Who helped you do the homework?" or "Maybe we ought to declare a holiday! Russell did his homework!" Sarcastic comments are expressions of hostility. Such expressions corrupt teacher-student dialogue, impair students' feelings of self-worth, and totally eliminate the possibility of a positive teacher-pupil relationship.

Parents repeatedly describe their work-inhibited children as overly sensitive and threatened by disapproval. Eric was one such child.

Eric's parents reported that their son was so distraught over his perception that his fourth-grade teacher did not like him that he was having trouble sleeping. The teacher was very concerned over Eric's repeated failure to complete almost any assignment and she had no difficulty describing her frustration. She was having no success, however, in helping Eric become a better student.

Her frustration was understandable, but what was more interesting was her expression of positive feelings toward Eric. "I really like him. He's sweet, pleasant and I worry because he seems so sad."

When she heard about Eric's negative feelings, his teacher was shocked. After consultation with the school's guidance counselor, she developed a new plan for Eric. She became more matter-of-fact about completion of assignments. She gave up her scolding behavior, began giving more attention to Eric apart from work, and reduced the frequency of her comments about his work. She also focused on being friendlier, and Eric began to relax.

Within a month, Eric's parents reported a change in their son's attitude toward school. "I think Mrs. Hunter likes me more than she used to." The change in the pattern of communication between teacher and student had good results. Eric's demeanor improved and he began to complete a few more assignments.

QUIET, MATTER-OF-FACT APPROACH

Many work-inhibited students feel particularly anxious, frightened, and resentful in the company of adults who yell. Work inhibition is so frustrating to parents and teachers that they are bound to feel like exploding. But the more teachers yell, the more counterproductive the yelling becomes. The same may be said for parents and other instructors.

Yelling is helpful in calling hogs, communicating across a football field, and in an emergency—but not in close proximity to others. And it certainly is inappropriate when the goal is to build a relationship with a child who lacks confidence, who is overly sensitive to threat, and who needs to experience comfort in his or her workplace.

Ask students to identify negative teacher behaviors and yelling will invariably be brought up. Many teachers believe that yelling is the only way to get the students' attention. But it is not.

Instead of yelling, try a benevolent silence. Avoid the "teacher stares" that the kids laugh about. Ask the students to relax, get comfortable, put their feet on the floor, smile. Use pleasant eye contact, walk around the room, stand next to the student who is most likely to be noisy.

Instead of standing and yelling, move to another spot. Stand in the back of the room and observe the students. They will turn around to see what's happening. The point is, do something other than yelling. If it is important to be loud, do so when you're happy!

BE GENUINE

In all communications with insecure work-inhibited students, it is important to be positive. But it is also important to be _genuine_. Express concern and interest only to the extent felt. When a teacher cannot be honestly positive and interested in his or her interactions with a work-inhibited student, it may be in the student's best interests for the teacher to recruit someone else to be the child's ally.

In any case, do not pretend interest and do not compliment a child when it is not meant. The danger of false communication is that it may reinforce the child's negative personal beliefs. "I must be pretty bad. The teacher has to make up things in order to say anything good about me."

One more point about providing extra attention and support for work-inhibited students at school: It is not an easy task. The students' problems are often of long standing, and it may take a long time to break through. Do not expect to see short-term results, but be assured that work-inhibited students do progress with nurturing from their teachers.

About Work

Work-inhibited students need help in learning persistence— to stay on task, to withstand failure, and to forge ahead. They need to learn the skills of stick-to-it-iveness more than academic skills.

Most work-inhibited students give up before they make any true effort. Many may work on their own for only a few minutes before they lay down their pencils and do almost anything except the assigned task.

Consider the case of Dan, a fifth-grader. Like many work-inhibited students, Dan often completed in-class assignments that required one- or two-word responses to short questions. He independently performed work that required about two minutes of his time. But Dan had great difficulty writing in his journal—even as much as a paragraph—and, especially, any lengthy writing task, such as a book report. Dan had some success in completing math computation exercises. But complex word problems that required him to read, analyze, and work through three or four stages to completion were an impossibility for him. All in all, Dan completed about 60 percent of the work assigned to him during the school day and turned in one out of five homework assignments.

Dan was successful in completing his art projects and he consistently worked hard to improve his excellent soccer skills. So it was evident that Dan was able to persist in some of his endeavors—but not in his basic academic work.

Dan's teacher carefully analyzed his pattern of work completion and on-task behavior. It was clear to him that Dan needed to maintain persistence for about ninety minutes of every school day. This analysis put the problem in perspective for the teacher. His mental picture of Dan changed from a problem child to a nice guy who was willing to learn, but who lacked the emotional strength to put forth sustained, independent effort in the completion of his school assignments.

Dan and his teacher already had a positive relationship. Now his teacher needed to use this relationship to help Dan do his work. The first step was to set up a meeting with Dan to identify the problem and establish a plan for helping him persevere.

MENTORS

Imagine a running back who has injured his knee. After surgery, he must rehabilitate his leg to develop the strength necessary to once again be an explosive runner. At first, with his muscles atrophied from disuse, the player suffers pain when walking, and he has doubts and experiences fear. Specialists tell the player he can recover, can once again carry the ball in competition, but that it will take hard work, extra effort, and sacrifice.

How is it possible for the professional athlete to work so hard, to produce so much effort for so many days to achieve his goal? For one thing, he has already experienced the rewards of success, and that in itself is a powerful motivator. He believes in his abilities and has learned to work hard to achieve his success. He is also supported by experts who assure him that he will recover. And he is given help in developing a program of rehabilitation.

In this player's corner are his wife, family, friends, fellow players, coaches, trainers, and doctors. He is counseled by a sports psychologist who helps him interpret and banish negative, self-defeating feelings. The player spends each day at his team's training facility, where he receives close, supportive supervision.

In one of his exercises, he must push against resistant devices. At first he is only able to move weights that a child could easily lift. His trainer yells encouragement: "You can do it! Push, push, push. Make it hurt! That's great! Way to go!"

The trainer records each day's activities. The daily log enables the player to see each bit of progress or lack of it. Likewise, the orthopedic surgeon keeps records and shares all his information with the player.

Like the athlete, work-inhibited students need to build up their strength to give extra effort. Unlike the athlete, work-inhibited students have never known success and do not believe in their abilities. This makes it even harder for them to succeed or even to stay on the task.

Nevertheless, the same principles that apply to the injured athlete apply to work-inhibited students. Work-inhibited students need the supportive help of an important adult—a mentor. Like the trainer who guides the rehabilitation program for the professional football player, a teacher or counselor may become a mentor for devising, coordinating, supervising, and encouraging a work-inhibited student through a program of mutual acceptance.

If it were possible to quantify student effort accurately, teachers could keep records on the amount of effort each student gives each day, week, or grading period. Charts might be kept that detailed if a student's efforts were increasing or decreasing. It would be possible to compare the quality and quantity of students' products with the amount of effort extended. If that were possible, the records would likely confirm what we already know—some students give modest effort while producing excellent products, and work-inhibited students must put forth considerable effort before they produce much at all.

It stands to reason that if it were easy for work-inhibited students to do their work, they would. But for them, just to stay on task independently, to write or to do math problems requires more than average effort.

Work-inhibited students need to know someone is on their side, someone who understands not only their problems, but their strengths. It is useful for teachers and counselors to communicate directly to them just what these strengths and weaknesses are. Through dispassionate description, teachers may enable students to feel less threatened by thoughts of how awful they are, because they also hear their good points articulated. An accurate description of the problem is the first step in solving it.

Dan's mentor was his teacher. In one of their meetings, the teacher provided an analysis: "Dan, I've been studying your performance for the past several weeks. It's clear to me that you have good reading skills. Your scores on the math placement test show that you have excellent math reasoning skills, and you have mastered almost all math skills expected for someone your age. In class your participation is usually pretty good.

"In your attempts to become a better student, you need help in staying on task to complete your class assignments—especially writing assignments. I want you to let me help you move in that direction."

It is important for work-inhibited students to be part of the plan and to experience the teacher/mentor's supportive help through frequent conferences about the amount of work completed. Schedule conferences at least once a week to discuss the tangible results of the students' efforts. Put forth some ideas as to what might be helpful. Encourage work-inhibited students to develop their own strategies to improve their own efforts. It is also important to ask students what assistance may have been beneficial in the past or if they have any suggestions for what might help now.

During the conference it is very useful for the teacher or counselor to convey a sense of positive expectations. Statements of positive expectations need not be grandiose. Instead a quiet assurance that academic and other pursuits will turn out all right often works well. "By our working together, perhaps you will find it easier to complete assignments and improve your writing skills."

Work-inhibited students need these messages of acceptance and positive expectation, since they have so little faith in themselves. Often they look at a lengthy assignment and think, "Oh, my! That's so long. It's too hard." Their thinking may include negative self-talk that paints a picture of current and future failure. Educators may help by projecting hope and by scrupulously avoiding lectures about the future consequences of not completing work.

Conference time should be as nonthreatening to the student as possible. The conferences may be used not only to plan programs of assistance, but also to review and chart progress. Engage the student in dialogue as to why certain assignments may be more difficult than others. In using information to modify future assignments, help to be given, and appropriate learning materials, send messages such as: "Keep trying, give a good effort." "It's okay, you're going to get better at this."

The emphasis should be on persistence, the amount of time spent working, and the quantity of work completed, in contrast to focusing on the number of correct answers. Count the problems worked on, the number of words written, or the paragraphs or pages completed. Of course, all students need help in knowing and understanding the subject matter, but for work-inhibited students, it is most effective to begin by recording and rewarding their efforts to do work.

WORKING INCREMENTALLY

Like the football player recovering from a serious knee injury, progress in helping work-inhibited students is likely to be slow. At first the child may respond positively to the special attention offered and show a dramatic improvement—a great start, but perhaps a false one, followed by a decline. Or the child may at first become even less efficient and then show some improvement. Progress may be made, but it is likely to be slow and certainly not always steady.

Rather than feeling defeated by the student's slow growth to competence, the teacher may take on the challenge—and it is a challenge—of accepting the fact that a work-inhibited student is not likely to do as much work as the average student and that he or she will need concentrated help for a long period of time. The teacher may need to set more modest sights on the amount of any assignment a work-inhibited student is likely to be able to complete.

If a general class assignment includes twenty problems, the teacher may judge that on a good day a certain work-inhibited student may complete seven. While other students may routinely write fifty- to seventy-word paragraphs, a work-inhibited student may only be able—with a good prompt—to write a sentence or two. In each case it is helpful to give a work-inhibited student assignments that may be completed with reasonable effort.

Just as it is true that students may have differing reading comprehension skills or differing abilities to solve math problems, students may have varying abilities in being able to complete assignments independently. It is as useful to encourage continued effort for those children who lag behind as it is for those who possess excellent working skills. And just as reading assignments may be varied according to an individual's reading skills, there is a need to vary assignments according to amount of productivity.

Is it permissible to vary assignments, to expect less from certain students while demanding more from others? Is it fair to allow certain students to do less? Why should Sandra be required to write paragraph after paragraph and to turn in all of her homework, while Mike completes very little homework and then gets extra attention for doing such a limited amount? The answer is that students who put forth extended effort in the completion of assignments grow in their own knowledge, skills, self-confidence, and ability to sustain effort. The student who works harder reaps many rewards and is thus encouraged to continue good efforts. The student who is able to complete assignments receives positive feedback, and the student who is incapable of putting forth effort independently needs to be encouraged to begin to work, to give effort, to risk making mistakes. A competent student is not likely to be discouraged because the teacher gives more help to the needy.

Teachers may choose among a variety of strategies. Sometimes an entire class may have the same assignment—which a work-inhibited student may well be able to complete if it is broken down into small, incremental steps. As the student completes each part, the teacher gives a pat on the back, a bit of encouragement—an emotional "pick-me-up"—to proceed on to the next step. The teacher tries to extend the student just a little bit.

This method is much like training to run faster. Runners set intervals during which they run hard and fast for a brief period, and then recover. Then they repeat the pattern. The goal is to run faster for short distances and then gradually extend the distance.

Teachers may ask work-inhibited students to give concentrated effort for a short period of time, followed by relaxation and a bit of nurturing. Slowly, the teacher enables the student to become more adept at putting forth effort for longer periods of time.

Varying the approach helps. Students like novelty. Surprise the child by insisting that only three questions be completed. Set up a challenge to work quickly. Use a timer and ask the student to beat the clock. Highlight or underline certain items and ask the student only to finish those that are so marked.

Maintain a careful record of assignments completed and graph the results. Student and teacher alike may be surprised and positively reinforced by viewing a graph that shows progress.

Do not let the work pile up. At the end of each period, go on to the next activity. If possible, collect any work, both complete and incomplete, and go on. Work-inhibited students easily feel overwhelmed and are unlikely to tackle a tableful of incomplete assignments. They do need to learn to tackle longer and longer assignments, but it is foolish to encourage work-inhibited students to climb a mountain when they are still unable to scale a hill.

Working incrementally means always taking it one day at a time. It means the teacher is pleased to see a work-inhibited student increase effort 100 percent when going from two minutes to four minutes, while most of the other students are able to work independently for half an hour. Bit by bit, focusing on successes, breaking assignments into smaller units, giving assignments that may be completed—this is the direction in which success lies.

Helping Hands

Most work-inhibited students will work with help. But a teacher with twenty-five students in a classroom can spend only a fraction of the day being next to and assisting any one individual. Therefore it may be useful to recruit helpers to assist work-inhibited students.

PEER SUPPORT

The classmates of work-inhibited students may be a rich resource. Pair classmates and encourage them to assist each other.

This technique is especially helpful for certain types of homework assignments. Imagine sending two fifth-graders to the library to find out about the Armenian holocaust, rather than asking each to investigate individually that historical episode. Peers working together minimize the pain of some schoolwork, while promoting learning and cooperation for both.

COOPERATION, NOT COMPETITION

In some classrooms, teachers discourage students working together for fear that one student may not do his or her fair share. Not only may cooperation be discouraged, but most classrooms are highly competitive and individual effort is rewarded highly. Competition may not be harmful to the winners, but the losses experienced by work-inhibited students only reaffirm their poor self-esteem and contribute to their continued failure.

In teaching work-inhibited students, cooperation and shared goals should be encouraged. Rather than emphasizing individual efforts, emphasis may be placed on group effort to create a climate of helpfulness. Early finishers of assignments may be encouraged to sit next to and help others who have more difficulty.

The teacher might teach all students how to be helpers, tutors, or teacher assistants. Imagine a classroom of learners in which all students are encouraged to help one another. Here a student with weak fine-motor and poor writing skills might receive help from another, who transcribes his thoughts onto paper. "It's my handwriting, but the ideas all belong to Chris."

CROSS-AGE TUTORING

Students enjoy helping each other. Older work-inhibited students often welcome the opportunity to tutor younger children. It not only adds variety to their day, but tutoring also helps them feel important. In high school, members of the National Honor Society, Key Club, or other service organizations may be ready and willing to give tutorial assistance. Each school is filled with helping hands.

ADULT VOLUNTEERS

Volunteers exist within the school and without. One teacher recruited three parent helpers to help one fourth-grade student who could not engage in lengthy writing projects. With the volunteers sitting next to him, this student began writing. The volunteers not only made it possible for the student to complete his work; he also improved his language arts skills.

Volunteers may be individuals other than parents. The parent-teacher organization may maintain a pool of concerned volunteers. Senior citizens groups may also provide an untapped fund of skilled helpers.

For some individuals, the use of fellow students, parents, and other volunteers in a program of supportive afternoon help might eliminate the nightly homework horrors that so often occur in the homes of work-inhibited students. Just removing this one major source of friction and attacks on self-esteem may contribute to easier successes.

PROFESSIONAL RESOURCE PROGRAMS

Schools can also consider hiring professionals or paraprofessionals to give supportive, nurturing assistance to small groups of willing work-inhibited students. If held after school, these activities should not be developed or seen as a punitive intervention. Rather, the help should be *offered* to students who want to be successful, but who just have a hard time doing homework on their own.

Programs may be developed during school hours where professionals help work-inhibited students. In one school system, a junior high guidance counselor was employed part-time—three periods each day—to work with just twenty-two students. The students met each day with the counselor (seven or eight children in each forty-five-minute period). With parental approval all the students elected to meet with the counselor in lieu of another subject or study hall. The goal of this resource program was to enable students with severe work-inhibition problems to become more effective in the completion of schoolwork. (See Appendix G.)

The program was successful. The positive impact of the program undoubtedly had a great deal to do with the attitude of the counselor/teacher, who responded to each of the students in an accepting, supportive, positive, and cheerful manner.

The class worked much like a study hall, but with just a few students helped by one teacher. Most of the class time was devoted to the completion of English, math, science, and social studies assignments.

Counseling was also provided to the students. This guidance helped them gain insight into the characteristics that inhibited their own ability to persist and to complete schoolwork. Counseling was ongoing and placed unobtrusively into the daily routine. There were no long individual sessions. Instead, the counselor/teacher used momentary opportunities to listen and to give feedback to students. The process enabled students to feel less pressure and to begin to develop a sense of mastery.

The emphasis was on what the student had to do that day and what might be accomplished. Students practiced simple organizational skills and were able to feel good as they checked off on their lists the assignments completed. Threats were never used. Instead, the focus was always on staying the course, keeping at it and not quitting.

Of course, the students did not always work and did not suddenly become proficient. There were the expected ups and downs. But in response to failure, the teacher would always convey a positive attitude. "It's okay, you'll get it tomorrow." "You're going to be okay."

Students enjoyed the resource program because they liked the teacher and because it made their lives easier. Their parents were happy, too, since many of them felt that at last the school system was doing something for their children. It was no small matter to be able to eliminate the nightly homework wars. Teachers were happy, since they had someone to help them with one of their biggest problems.

Resource programs may be successful in almost any school, if they follow certain rules:

- Student groups must be small enough to enable the teacher to make contact with each student every few minutes.
- Students must want the program for themselves and elect to enroll.
- The teacher must not be demanding or negative. Rather, he or she must nurture, encourage, and support students' efforts, even when those efforts are almost negligible.

Ongoing small group or tutorial help enables many work-inhibited students to experience persistence—on-task behavior that results in the completion of academic products. These products are powerful reinforcers that improve the poor self-esteem of work-inhibited students.

ELIMINATE NEGATIVE, PUNISHING COMMENTS;
USE POSITIVE REINFORCEMENT

Educational researcher Ned Flanders has developed highly precise techniques called "interaction analysis" to observe classroom interactions. What he and his followers have observed is that teachers are much more likely to give their students negative rather than positive feedback. In spite of the almost universally held academic belief that appropriate positive comments are more effective than negative ones, children are still more likely to be criticized than praised. These negative comments are not necessarily punitive or inappropriate; in Flanders's studies, a teacher acknowledging an answer as wrong is a negative response. Nevertheless, teachers may improve their effectiveness by increasing the frequency of positive responses while reducing the negative.

✳ Providing positive, effective feedback to students is not necessarily easy. For praise to be effective, certain rules should be remembered. Reward the *action* or *product* with positive attention, not the *person*. Comment specifically about what it is the student has accomplished. Comments should not be exaggerated or insincere, but rather true and to the point. "Nineteen out of twenty correct! You really understand!" "Your use of shading in this painting gives the scene perspective and a sense of distance." "Your paragraph included three funny examples of what can happen on the first day of school." "Joe, your speech kept everyone's attention."

Avoid at all costs unnecessary negative comments when speaking to a work-inhibited student. If Abe is engaging in a negative behavior that is not harmful to him or others (daydreaming rather than doing a writing assignment, for instance), avoid correcting or saying something like, "Abe, are you going to do anything this morning?" Productive options for the teacher may include helping or communicating positively with *another* nearby student, quietly standing or sitting next to Abe, or asking Abe if he needs any help.

Sometimes positive reinforcement does not require words. Just a smile or a pat on the back may keep a student working. What is important is to notice what the student is doing or has accomplished.

What is *not* effective is to make a global statement about

the quality of the person. If Beth has just completed a timed math test in a personal record time, the comment may be, "Beth, you have just set a new personal record. You really know your fives tables!" and not "Beth, what a terrific girl you are!"

As discussed earlier, work-inhibited students work best when a caring teacher is right beside them, makes a special effort to notice work-inhibited students, and communicates to them both acceptance and support.

In giving positive reinforcement, it is important to separate acceptance and caring from reward for effort. Show that you accept and care for the child, even when the effort given or work produced may not be worthy of recognition. It may not always be possible to give a student positive reinforcement for putting forth effort or producing work; yet it is possible to give a smile and a friendly hello. Caring for students should not be connected to performance.

If a teacher's positive reinforcement is to be effective, it must be true and accurate. Insincere praise can reinforce negative self-esteem. Imagine Kevin, a struggling Little Leaguer. There is usually a Kevin on every Little League team—the weakest player who only sees action because league rules require that every child play in every game. Kevin may not have gotten a hit all season and he usually strikes out. So Kevin comes to the plate and the coach yells encouragement. "C'mon, Kevin. Get a hit! Let's go, big fella! This one's yours!"

Everyone is rooting for Kevin, just hoping he will not strike out again. Kevin swings and weakly taps the ball back to the pitcher who easily throws Kevin out at first base. In response, the coach does not say to Kevin, as he might to the others, "Get 'em next time!" Instead, he yells, far too loudly, "Good effort! Way to go, Kevin! Good wood on the ball!" Kevin can't help but think, "Boy, am I bad! He yells that even when I barely got the ball back to the pitcher."

With the technique of positive reinforcement, what is *not*

said may be as important as what *is* said. When the child is not doing what he is supposed to, use as few words as possible. On the other hand, communicate positively and frequently whenever the child performs even a small behavior in the direction of work completion.

Whenever possible, ignore negative behaviors and attend to the positive. Imagine a group of students working—all but one. Rather than call attention to the one nonproductive student, it may be useful instead to notice nearby working students. It is possible that the attention showed to the workers may spur the nonworker to be productive in order to gain for him or herself the teacher's interest.

When giving positive attention, do not spoil the positive message with qualifiers. Too often the compliment is ruined by such add-ons as, "That's good work, today! Excellent penmanship. Now why can't you always do that?" "Jennifer, see how well you can do when you try?" "Tom, you finished the book. It's about time!"

When noting positive behavior or products, just give the specific message. Do not remind the child that he or she usually does not do well, did not do well yesterday, and is not likely to do well again.

Teachers are not the only ones who may give positive reinforcement. Everyone in the class might do it! Encourage classmates to support each other by modeling positive communication. Furthermore, teachers may positively reinforce positive student-to-student comments. The goal is to create a climate of encouragement.

Confident Expectations

While positive reinforcement should be tied specifically to real efforts and accomplishments, no matter how the child performs, it is always useful to convey messages of confident expectations. Children benefit from feelings of hope, not despair.

Worry is the culprit. Teachers and parents are so concerned about the future consequences of not doing schoolwork that they naturally share their concerns. How many children have heard, "If you don't do your schoolwork, you won't get into college." "You won't amount to anything if you don't do your work." Day in and day out, work-inhibited students are reminded of the likelihood of continued failure, thereby fueling feelings of hopelessness and low self-esteem.

Teachers are not prone to remind successful students that their work is due. Nor are they likely to say, "If you don't work hard, you won't be successful." Instead, a quiet assurance prevails that reinforces confidence. When adults believe in their children, they are not as likely to give reminders to do or admonitions for not doing. Teachers believe in successful students and convey those assurances in words and through nonverbal communication. In return, successful students continue to grow in confidence and competence.

If it works for successful students, maybe the same messages should be given to those less able. Work-inhibited students need to hear, "Don't worry. You will get it." "You're going to be successful." "You're okay, just hang in there." It is useful to minimize the reminders and lectures. Instead give smiles and nods of encouragement and messages of trust and positive expectations.

Empower the Child

Some children come to kindergarten and first grade feeling pretty good about themselves and continue to possess those positive feelings throughout their school years. On the other hand, work-inhibited students need all the help they can get in order to bolster their weak egos. One way to help is to give these students power.

To be empowered is to be able to take care of oneself and to have influence on others. It is useful for educators to empower children to make decisions for themselves, to be given adult-like responsibilities, and to be given opportunities for leadership.

RECOGNITION WITH RESPONSIBILITY

Some school systems institutionalize programs that empower children—for example, safety patrols. When a student becomes a patrol, he or she holds the responsibility for the safety of others and the opportunity to exercise leadership with peers. With this position goes considerable recognition. The patrol leader not only has a badge, but is often let out of class early.

Patrols may be honored in the school or community with parades, free tickets to see the local team, or banquets. Everyone is impressed—including fellow students, parents, and younger siblings.

While it is not possible for every work-inhibited student to be a patrol every year, it is possible to empower them in other ways. Teachers need helpers to clean the blackboard, to run errands, to pass out papers, to monitor younger students, to run the copying machine.

Students not only enjoy the diversion of doing something different, they feel good about themselves when they are singled out and are able to do a good job. These jobs are sometimes made even more important when given special titles or other recognition.

In junior and senior high schools, work-inhibited students may be aides to the secretarial staff in the guidance and administrative offices. Students are used by teachers to help in labs, shops, and the library. Work-inhibited students are excellent candidates for school jobs, since they thrive on the opportunity for diversity in their day, as well as the recognition they earn for engaging in important work.

Giving work-inhibited students opportunities to be involved

and to contribute promotes their attachment to their school and their feelings of self-worth. For example, one school's athletic director recruited a group of students each year to assist in the maintenance of playing fields and equipment. These boys were invariably work-inhibited in academics.

This group early on became known as Arnie's Army and everyone was aware that they could always be counted on to discharge their responsibility. Each member of Arnie's Army knew his way around and could be trusted with keys and expensive equipment. The coaching staff would rely on members of Arnie's Army to help with inventory and to assist during emergencies. Members had a certain style and a place of importance in the school. No matter how poor their classroom performance, these boys were not about to drop out. They were too important to the school, and they knew it!

DECISION-MAKING

Another important facet of feeling empowered relates to decision-making. In high school, students have opportunities to make important decisions as to what courses they will take and what career paths they may embark on. At all levels, it is important to empower students to make decisions regarding daily activities, including how to accomplish tasks and what is to be studied. Being asked "What do you think?" or "What do you want to do?" imparts a sense of importance to students and fuels their sense of control and independence. The goal is to promote autonomy so that students may stand on their own and feel good about their own sense of adequacy.

It Is Okay to Make Mistakes

Work-inhibited students tend to avoid some tasks because they fear failure. They do not realize that failure is normal and necessary for learning. These students need to modify their thinking about schoolwork—that it is okay to make mistakes, that it is even beneficial to make errors when developing new skills and knowledge.

Teachers are often poor models for the value of failure. It is not hard to imagine a second-grade student believing the teacher never makes mistakes. Furthermore, teachers reward perfection, not sloppy papers and misspelled words.

MISTAKES ARE PART OF LEARNING

It is important to *teach* students how to cope with failure. Students may remember their early failures in learning to ride a bike or a skateboard, or learning to swim. Hold class discussions about how mistakes are made while learning new tasks, both in and out of school.

Students may study how famous people learned to cope with and benefit from failure. Discussions may be held about popular movies in which heroes come back from repeated adversity and prevail by not giving up.

TEACHERS MODEL OWN MISTAKES

Teachers may be positive models by pointing out their own mistake-making. Teachers may say, "I didn't do that correctly." "I made a mistake." "I can't solve this problem. I guess I need more information." "The way I'm doing this is not working. I wonder how I might do it differently."

Through modeling, teachers can show students that it is okay to try, emphasizing the importance of effort, not perfect papers.

Clear Guidelines

While it is clear that work-inhibited students need special attention, the guidelines and rules established by schools governing student grades and behavior should generally be the same as for other students. Students benefit from understanding what they need to learn and what tasks they must complete. Students, parents, and teachers need to know what the objectives of the learning process are and to what extent these objectives have been achieved.

For work-inhibited children, special care must be taken in separating how well the child has mastered knowledge and skills from the issues of persistence, hard work, and the quantity of classwork and homework completed and submitted to the teacher. It is important that ongoing evaluation of students' progress include the amount of time and effort the students give to the learning process.

Since success is dependent upon hard work, the amount of effort given needs to be evaluated. Just as it is important to evaluate skills in math, reading, and knowledge of world events, it is also important to assess students' work behaviors.

As for the rules of the school governing student conduct and behavior, work-inhibited students do not need special exceptions. Talking out, skipping class, being tardy or disrespectful are no more acceptable for work-inhibited students than for any others. All students and classrooms benefit from clearly defined rules that promote classroom decorum and prevent the abuse of any one person by another. To make exceptions for work-inhibited students may send a message that they are less capable than their peers.

Practices to Avoid

Certain educational practices seem to be detrimental to work-inhibited students. These include requiring a child to repeat a given grade for failure to complete assignments, restricting a student from participating in one activity for failure to do well at another, persistently keeping a child in from recess for not doing class assignments, and blaming the parents for the child's ineffectiveness.

RETENTION

The outcomes of retention, or holding a child back to repeat a grade, are often extremely negative. Children often view repeating a grade as catastrophic—an indictment, a confirmation of failure. For some, being retained exacerbates feelings of low self-esteem, thus making it even *more* difficult for the child to overcome problems of work inhibition.

The negative impact of retention appears to increase the later retention occurs in a child's school life. Delaying a child's entrance into kindergarten one year is usually less problematic than having him or her repeat kindergarten or first grade. Failure to be promoted in later elementary grades or high school is often devastating to a youngster.

Parents and teachers may recommend retention for work-inhibited students, believing the extra year might enable the student to become more mature. Since many work-inhibited children have good cognitive abilities and therefore good learning potential, it is natural to think that these children just need more time. But what work-inhibited students need is not more of the same. They need new, additional kinds of supportive help.

ELIMINATING EXTRACURRICULAR ACTIVITIES

The most enriching part of school life for some children occurs away from instruction in the basic skills and disciplines. Being part of a school play, belonging to a computer club, engaging in athletics, being a safety patrol, serving as a class officer, and engaging in other activities are invaluable learning and living experiences.

When remembering childhood experiences, who recalls third-grade reading, after all? But almost anyone would remember with pleasure being chosen to represent the school on the championship gymnastics team or singing a solo at the winter pageant or being selected for the district-wide orchestra.

It does not make sense to restrict valuable opportunities due to poor performance in school. Indeed, just the opposite is what should happen! Educators—and parents—should seek opportunities for work-inhibited children to succeed away from their usual failure experiences. If a child who will not do math will do art, give the child art. The struggle to improve in math may be less difficult, and the student's sense of self-worth may improve as the paintings are viewed by all. And phrasing math problems in art terms might enhance the appeal of math as well!

DENYING RECESS

More than one parent has lamented that it does not seem right or useful to keep their child inside nearly every day while others enjoy the release of recess. Almost any child will assert that recess is the best part of the school day.

Since recess is pleasurable, teachers have often found it useful to say, "If you don't finish your work now, you will have to do it during recess." Many students do hurry to complete their work in time to experience fun and relief from schoolwork. If a student occasionally misses recess, and the practice of denying recess to those who do not do their work does enable students to be more persistent, and if this practice keeps children working, then it may be a good idea to continue that practice.

On the other hand, if a work-inhibited student rarely goes to recess and the teacher continually loses a needed break, give it up! The technique isn't working, after all. Recess may be less valuable as a tool of discipline and more valuable as a respite and time for the child to regain the energy to participate in other learning activities.

BLAMING PARENTS

Considerable tact and care need to be employed by teachers when communicating with parents of work-inhibited students.

Parents undoubtedly worry even more than teachers about the horrible outcomes of their child not doing schoolwork.

It does no good to blame parents, to suggest that it is their fault that Johnny or Denise doesn't stay on task. What is needed is a partnership of teacher and parents, an opportunity to meet and to consider together what to do to help. Cooperation between teachers and parents is essential to coordinate parallel responses for the child at home and at school.

Educators must be very careful in calling or sending messages to parents about their children's failure to complete homework. When a teacher calls to say, "Alan has not been completing his class and homework assignments," the implication is that the parent has a responsibility for doing something—to make Alan do his work. In most instances work inhibition is a long-term problem that parents have been trying to solve for years. With a call from the teacher, parents may feel even more pressure. It is their fault. They have to do something.

So when a call must be made to parents of work-inhibited students, teachers probably best serve students like Alan by conveying empathy: "I know you have been trying to help Alan." Do not demand that the parents do something to Alan to make him do his work. Request that the parents meet with the teachers and guidance counselors, school psychologists, and perhaps administrators to design plans for school and home.

A Plan for Schools

In the best of all possible worlds, teachers of work-inhibited students have broad support from their principals. Work-inhibited students have their best chance when they are enrolled in schools that have systematically developed interventions to help them overcome their emotional inhibitions to do the work of school.

Within their classrooms, teachers function in a rather autonomous fashion. While they may institute the recommendations described in this book, they are more likely to be
successful in their efforts if they have the support of fellow
teachers, counselors, psychologists, and, most importantly,
their principals.

There are no quick fixes that enable work-inhibited students
to become academically competent. Positive outcomes are best
realized with positive educational practices that remain in
place year after year, from teacher to teacher, with the help
and support of parents, counselors, psychologists, and
administrators.

It is possible for any school to become more responsive to
the needs of work-inhibited students. Changes for the better
begin with clear identification of the problem. The first step
is to collect solid data that define which students have difficulty
completing school assignments. When work inhibition becomes obvious to members of the staff, it is possible to determine what is and is not true about such students. As the
characteristics of work-inhibited students are better understood, educators may consider which educational practices are
useful and which are not.

Any member of a school staff may systematically begin a
process of change. It may be a guidance counselor who is interested in getting the school to develop strategies to help
work-inhibited students. He or she may begin by letting others
know of this interest, to recruit interested parties to collect
information on how many students exist within the school who
routinely fail to engage in or complete their schoolwork. The
process of collecting information brings to light the magnitude
of the problem.

As the problem becomes accepted as important, it often becomes useful to bring additional consultants or experts into
the school from the outside. These experts from the fields of
education or psychology may not only add information, but

may also facilitate the process of changing existing practices. A planning leader from outside the system may have expertise that will be accepted more easily by a group of individuals holding divergent viewpoints about how best to help students become more productive. This process should improve communication among teachers, administrators, and parents.

Finally, action steps may be developed. The staff may develop an understanding and begin practicing the communicative, constructive, positive behaviors that are in the best interests of work-inhibited students. Such practices need to be continually encouraged by principals, thus enabling teachers to persist in working with the work-inhibited students who require such sustained help.

The next chapter presents recommended parenting responses that support their work-inhibited children's growth into competence. Teachers as well as parents may find these suggestions helpful; they are designed to complement the recommendations offered for school.

7 / How Parents Can Help Their Work-Inhibited Children

An effective regimen has been developed for parents to help children overcome work inhibition. If followed, children and their parents are likely to feel better and do better. The recommended actions do not make life more complex or difficult; rather, interactions between parents and children should become simpler and more pleasant. It should also be remembered, however, that long-existing patterns of work inhibition change only gradually.

Consider the problem of work inhibition as it might exist with children of ten years or more. First, though the origins begin early in life, the problem is not likely to be identified until the child is in third or fourth grade. Thus, certain personality traits that relate to work inhibition are well entrenched before the problem is tackled by parents, teachers, or counselors. Second, work-inhibited students typically have strengths—they can be warm, engaging, and often intellectually able—yet in spite of their strengths, they are very dependent. Work-inhibited students have not grown apart from their parents and become independent. Third, and most profoundly, these students are insecure. They have poor academic self-esteem. Finally, work-inhibited children are quietly resistant, not only to doing their schoolwork, but also to following through on their responsibilities at home. These children are often masters at hooking their parents into battles over preparing for school, doing chores, or getting ready for bed.

Without guidance and support, parents are alone in their attempts to help their work-inhibited children. It is not surprising that parents "try everything" to get them to do their work. Unfortunately their efforts typically exacerbate the problem. Rather than helping their children become more independent, parents become overly involved and promote further dependence. With misguided advice—"he's just lazy, and he could do it if he wanted to"—parents may also be prone to act critical, demanding, and angry with their work-inhibited children.

While acknowledging that there are no quick fixes for work inhibition, the recommendations in this chapter show parents how to help their children become independent, self-sufficient, and, indeed, happier. The first section focuses on changing counterproductive patterns of communication between parents and children, thus strengthening family relationships. As work-inhibited children realize the affection of and acceptance by their parents, they are likely to be more receptive to other help their parents might offer. In the second section, parents are shown how to promote their children's growth from dependence to independence. In the third section, parents are advised how to nurture and reinforce assertiveness in their all-too-often passive, work-inhibited children. The final section of the chapter offers techniques for parents on how to improve their work-inhibited children's proficiency in completing tasks at home and school.

Strengthening Family Relationships

AFFECTION

Affection is a fundamental building block of a child's sense of security. Articulated as well as nonverbal expressions of caring—not simply when a child does something special, but also just for being—provide the emotional strength for a child to develop positive self-esteem.

Parents should consider the dynamics of relationships among father, mother, and their work-inhibited children. If family relationships are relatively harmonious, expressions of affection and acceptance may be given frequently and in an unqualified manner. Conversely, it is difficult for there to be harmony and free expression of affection when a state of tension and anger exists. To the extent that work-inhibited children live with discord in the family, their opportunities for growth to success are limited. These children need their parents' expressions of affection to fuel their own growth to self-sufficiency.

There is no one simple formula as to how each parent should give affection. Everyone has his or her own style, personality, and ways of communicating. What is important, however, is to convey to children that they are loved and cared for. Period. Not because they cleaned their rooms, brushed their teeth, or because they are attractive. It is crucial to bestow expressions of affection *just because they are our children.*

"I will love you no more or less because you please or displease me." "I love and care for you, whatever happens." Children benefit from knowing that they will be cared for and loved, no matter what their performance in school. It is not enough for parents just to *have* these positive feelings. *They must be communicated verbally.*

In some families, hugs and kisses and loving words are shared often. In other families, these expressions are more subtle. The style may not be important, but *what is important is that children feel emotionally nurtured.* Affection may be expressed with hugs, smiles, pats on the head, friendly greetings, and being tucked into bed. Emotional nurturing may occur at family mealtime, snacks after school, or with notes tucked into lunchboxes.

Yes, this may seem obvious. But in our hurried world, it is easy to overlook the obvious. For those parents who are engaged in even minor conflicts with their children, it is possible that affectionate responses may dwindle from often to occasional or even seldom.

Of course, children are not always delightful, and it is normal to become angry when they do not help with household chores or work on school assignments. As conflicts grow, however, rifts in relationships increase. Warm, affectionate moments may become less frequent and increasingly difficult to achieve. Children begin to expect nagging and frequent reminders, sarcasm, and threats. These messages may result in further deterioration of relationships and weaken the child's chances for success.

Parents are generally aware that their frequent complaints are hurting their relationships. Said one parent:

> I don't want to be a nag, a constant source of unpleasantness. It's just that I worry and he just sits there and watches TV. His grades are awful. We have tried to do all the right things. Our son was never without our attention. We tried so hard. The teachers and counselors never seemed to really know what it was we were supposed to do. And what really bothers me now is to see our son drifting away from us.

Being a good student is important. But having good mental health and a good self-image are *more* important. The benefits of sharing positive relationships with parents remain throughout life, while many of the consequences of low grades may be overcome. How important are homework assignments and good grades, really? Even if animosity worked miracles in bringing about good grades, would it be worth it?

Depending upon the degree of estrangement, many parents of work-inhibited students may benefit from rethinking existing patterns of communication. Messages of endearment are a good place to begin. Giving affection should not be dependent on any given set of circumstances. Tension can be reduced and warmth increased with soft, warm hellos, friendly smiles, and long, affectionate hugs.

ACCEPTANCE

What a terrible feeling it must be for a child to believe he or she is not the person his or her parents wanted. Acceptance, shown by affection, can counteract those feelings.

A proud father spoke about his fifteen-year-old son:

> I love sports, will play almost any game. When my son was born, I was thrilled. My first thoughts were about the two of us playing catch.
>
> Well, Chris is no athlete. He's never had much aptitude and couldn't care less. I tried to get him interested in sports and he does humor me, but it just isn't him.
>
> But he is interested in music. All kinds. Some of the stuff he plays, I can't get into. But he also is in a community symphony, plays in the school marching band, and writes music. It's wonderful! He's just great!

Work-inhibited children are particularly vulnerable to the feeling that they are not living up to their parents' expectations. They feel badly about their own school failures, and they know their problems are upsetting to their parents. Their fear of loss of parental acceptance is an emotional burden that hinders their ability to break out of their insufficiency. While parents certainly should avoid communicating that they approve of their children's lack of effort to do schoolwork, they should communicate their approval and acceptance of *other facets* of their children's interests and pursuits.

Of course, children do not always possess the traits, temperament, interests, or beliefs that parents hope for. While behavior that is self-destructive or harmful to others should be rejected and eliminated, children should have the right to be individuals. It is important to convey to children that they are unique, that they will grow apart from their parents, and that it is okay for corporate executives' children to become carpenters and for lovers of classical music to have children addicted to bluegrass. It is *not* necessary to be *wildly* enthusiastic about children's interests and activities, but it *is* unwise to condemn them.

Negative comments about mannerisms, body build, appearance, interests, and personality traits should be avoided. Just as children need affection, they need to receive the message that it is okay to be themselves, however they are, whatever they like, however they look. Such approval promotes comfort with separation from parents and growth toward independence.

LISTENING

There is probably no better way to convey acceptance than through listening! Quiet, attentive, reflective listening to what children have to say shows support and care. All parents have to do is put down their newspapers or turn down the television and become attentive. (Suggestions on attentive, reflective listening appear in Chapter 6.)

Parents should refrain from asking many questions— especially about school. It seems that every day, all across America, children receive the same after-school greeting: "Hi, honey! How was school? Do you have any homework?"

The response is standard, too. "Hi. Fine. No."

If a child does not share his or her thoughts very often, the best way to find out what's going on is to stop asking! And when a child actually discusses what is happening or what is of interest, parents should be calm and not overrespond—they should just listen.

It is okay to share "parental" thoughts, but only if requested. Parents should try not to evaluate, interrupt, warn, lecture, scold, or tell their own stories. Instead, they should pay attention and respond with something like, "It sounds as though you had a bad day." "It must be tough to have to face that every day." "How could you keep a straight face?" "That sounds awfully hard. Do you need my help?" "Let me know more when you find out what happens." "I'm glad you told me."

Parents who become attentive listeners may develop a new problem. Their kids may not stop talking! Think about it. Everyone loves an audience!

When a child starts really sharing, he or she may say something the parent is not ready for, or may tell about events or thoughts that are scary. The opportunity exists right there to be a wise and caring parent. Now is the time to *really* listen. It is rarely necessary—or valuable—for parents to *tell* their children what values and beliefs they possess. Children know already, because parents communicate these values through the manner in which they speak and act—indeed, the way they live their lives. If lecturing is minimized, then when parents must advise or say no, it is more likely that children will pay attention.

As work-inhibited children begin to enjoy a sharing relationship with their parents, they will also begin to experience a rebirth of their personal well-being. These positive feelings will have a salutary effect on their growth toward self-sufficiency.

PLAY

In the best of all possible worlds, couples decide to become parents for the pleasure of it all—to be part of the adventure of nurturing one's own through the many phases of childhood. What better way to be part of a child's life than through play! Play is joyful, exuberant, and often spontaneous. Parents should seize opportunities to engage in play activities that are within their children's interests and abilities. This is especially important for work-inhibited children, who need their parents' affection, acceptance, and guidance. These children not only feel nurtured through play; they also learn social skills that will enhance their relationships with peers.

And they should play for the *fun* of it! Play should be uncritical and have no emphasis on instruction. Play not only can bind relationships, but can improve muscle tone and agility, foster intellectual curiosity and knowledge, reduce tension, and impact positively on social skills.

Nonjudgmental, interactive participation nurtures a child's self-confidence. Imagine a six-year-old playing with blocks while Mom or Dad is in the room. The parent is nonintrusive, perhaps reading, folding laundry, or knitting. Occasionally the child makes a comment, and the two may engage in brief dialogue. At times the parent gives assistance, perhaps demonstrates, and always encourages. Here the child is playing independently with the support of a parent. At other times and with older children, play may be interactive, more complex, or highly structured (as in board games, cards, etc.). In these situations as well, parents should strive to be uncritical, good-humored, and supportive.

Work-inhibited children often have difficulty engaging in competitive play. They seem to enjoy themselves only when they are winning. Losing is threatening to their fragile self-esteem. If the game does not go their way, they may bend the rules to the displeasure of the other participants. They may be so lacking in confidence that they avoid playing with boys and girls their own age. Parents and teachers note that work-inhibited children often play with younger children, thereby reducing the risk of defeat or rejection.

When socially immature children have difficulty playing successfully with their peers, they need special help to master skills and overcome emotional inhibitions. Parents should play games with their children that are appropriate for their age. Parents may model positive sharing behaviors and offer occasional suggestions on how to improve skills.

It may also be helpful to invite another child to the home. Two children are much more likely to play successfully together than three or more. Parents should identify the friends with whom the child gets along well and those who have good social skills. These children should be paired up with the work-inhibited child. Socially adept children are often more forgiving, more likely to overlook minor irritations, and may also model appropriate behaviors.

Most parents enjoy playing alongside and with their children—not only to help them learn, but also just to have fun. Affectionate affiliation between parents and their children has been found to be a positive determinant for school achievement. Parental nurturing moves their child's growth toward positive self-esteem.

Play is good medicine in the effort to reduce tension, and in the homes of many severely work-inhibited children, a sense of high anxiety often prevails. Fearsome worry about the horrible outcomes of not doing schoolwork is difficult to dispel. There is little doubt, however, that the best way to effect positive change is to invest time and effort in improving family relationships. Parents should be affectionate, convey acceptance, listen to what their children have to say, and genuinely enjoy being with them through play and good humor.

Move to Autonomy: Setting Limits

Children who receive affection and messages of acceptance are likely to feel secure. As children grow, these feelings of security also need to grow beyond the children's relationships with their parents. Children need to be comfortable in their endeavors *apart* from Mom and Dad, to feel that it is indeed okay to be autonomous and separate.

One way for parents to help their children move toward autonomy is to set clear limits on negative behaviors. Parents who are able to practice effective, positive discipline help their children develop positive social skills and become independent. This is especially important for work-inhibited children, who are typically overly dependent upon the support of others to complete school assignments.

Effective discipline reduces tension and clarifies for children their role, responsibilities, and identity in the world. Effective discipline need not be complex; indeed, it ought to be quite simple. Effective discipline is neither harsh nor does it allow the child to rule the roost.

Some parents have trouble setting limits on the behavior and demands of their work-inhibited children for a number of reasons. Among the most common is the belief that an autocratic—rather than a democratic—approach to parenting is bad for the child. Other parents fear that they may displease, and therefore lose the love of, their children if they are too strict.

These fears notwithstanding, children need to know where their parents draw the line. Parents must communicate simply and clearly and consistently to their children just what is expected of them. This approach is most effective when mothers and fathers—together—give similar messages to their children.

In learning to become socially adept and confident, children as young as age three can learn appropriate rules of give-and-take from parents who establish clear guidelines for appropriate behavior. Most work-inhibited students have not internalized these rules. They fight to have their own way and to control their parents. On the following several pages are strategies for parents to set limits on their children's inconsiderate or infantile behaviors.

FEW RULES

Keep it simple. Family decorum is usually not well served by trying to enforce a multitude of rules and complicated procedures. The goal is to discourage behaviors that endanger one's safety and that are harmful to or inconsiderate of others. Helpful acts such as cleaning and straightening up should be encouraged. Children should also be encouraged to take care of themselves. A few guidelines are all that is needed: Be considerate of others, give a helping hand, be safe.

Specific rules are needed to protect children from danger: "Wear your seat belt." "Be home at a 'reasonable' hour." "Tell me where you are going and when you will be home."

Children should be encouraged to be considerate of others, to help out in the completion of household tasks, and to follow the directions of their parents. By and large, children learn how to take care of themselves and how to cooperate by following the examples and suggestions of their parents. A few specific rules governing the completion of household chores are typically useful. Children also need to know that it is not okay to be abusive to others.

BE ABLE TO SAY NO

Parents should not be too permissive or allow their children to have too much control over the household. Rather, when it is necessary to tell a child to do or not to do something, the child should be told simply and directly. "Tom, it is time for dinner. Come to the table." "Jenny, turn off the TV and gather your books together." "Zach and Molly, stop fighting."

It is important for parents to say no to negative behavior and to *direct their children to do what is expected.* What happens all too often is that work-inhibited children—and others—argue with their parents. "David, come in the house."

"Why?"

"Because it's time to get ready for bed."

"In a little bit."

"No, come in now."

"I'm just going to do this first."

"David, come at once!"

"Randy's mother doesn't make him come in."

"I don't care about Randy. Come in the house or you won't get any ice cream."

"I'll be there in just a minute."

Parents who allow their children to discuss, debate, and consider the pros and cons of each parental directive run the risk of overempowering their children (see Chapter 4). Overempowered children have excessive control over the household. They are permitted to wield as much power as their parents, or more. Furthermore, they usually become enmeshed emotionally with their parents and have difficulty separating psychologically. Such children are often considered spoiled because they expect their parents to be in service to their wishes.

Parents should say "no" just once. When children debate the merits of whether or not to do as they are told, parents must follow through with their requirements. Rather than provide reasons or plead with the child, David's parent should just go out and bring David in the house. If a child does not become quiet when told to, rather than argue with the child, take him to his room. Parents need to be in reasonable control and can do so by setting *and enforcing* reasonable and clear limits on the behavior of their children.

When enforcing rules, parents *need not* and generally *should not* be very talkative. While it is a good idea for parents to talk with their children under most circumstances, it is not effective to converse freely when setting limits on negative behaviors. Talking, trying to be persuasive, giving extended explanations, or arguing may reinforce negative behaviors. Parents will find it more useful to be strong and silent. In response to refusals and other negative behavior on the part of the children, there are at least four effective courses of action: ignore the behavior, separate the child from the scene, withdraw privileges, or have the child make amends.

IGNORE

One reason children upset and aggravate their parents is to grab attention. Parents actually fuel negative, attention-seeking behaviors by noticing them, since at times children will act obnoxious just to get Mom or Dad's attention. Ignoring helps not only to extinguish such behaviors as temper tantrums; it also permits a child to grow comfortably and separately from parents who do not focus on the child's every word or action.

Fortunately, most misbehavior is neither harmful nor dangerous, and much of it may be overlooked. But it is so easy for parents to comment on behaviors that indeed might, with a little mental effort, be ignored. "Don't whine." "Sit still." "Don't play with your food." "Leave your brother alone." So rather than making many comments, parents should practice ignoring.

SEPARATE THE CHILD FROM THE SCENE

Sometimes children (young or old) may be extremely bothersome, and it does no good to ignore them. Parents should remove the child or children from the scene—perhaps to their bedrooms.

Suppose Mark is fighting with his brother Adam or they are tearing the rec room apart. They should just be separated or moved. It does not have to be for a long time. Parents can say, "Come on out when you're able to get along or feel better." Again, actions often speak louder than words.

Another tactic parents may use with disruptive children is for the *parents* to leave. Without announcing, "I'm leaving," parents should move to another place in the house. It is often amazing how well siblings will get along when parents are not in view.

MAKING AMENDS

There may be natural consequences of certain negative behaviors. If a child breaks, damages, or destroys property belonging to another, the child—if old enough—should repair or replace it or else pay for its replacement.

Children should make amends when they hurt someone else's feelings. Parents are wise to tell a child about the need for apologies sometime *after* the heat of the negative incident has cooled. In any case, it is important for children to learn early to be cooperative, caring members of their family and community.

REMOVE PRIVILEGES

Parents may also withhold privileges important to the child. This tactic should be used with children who are old enough to understand the consequence. When a child does not come home at the time specified, it may be reasonable to use restriction and to keep the child home the following afternoon or Saturday night. If a daughter does not return or properly take care of clothes borrowed from Mom, do not lend her clothes for a specified time. The consequence of withholding the privilege should fit the offense.

Parents may restrict children's freedom and take away pleasurable opportunities and possessions when they have not acted in a manner that was understood or previously agreed upon. Judicious and occasional use of restriction may be helpful to a child who has *flagrantly* or *deliberately* engaged in harmful or dangerous acts or has been unable to follow reasonable limitations.

NO THREATS, NO SPANKING

Effective discipline should not be harmful to children. Punitive practices not only tend to be ineffective in changing children's behavior for the better; they also thwart positive parent-child relationships. Corporal punishment has been found to increase childhood aggression, reduce self-confidence, and increase anxiety.

Parents typically use threats and spankings when they feel powerless and angry. The use of this negative, impulsive punishment is inconsistent with what is desirable to teach children. It is far better for children to learn that the use of violence is not acceptable in solving problems.

In order for work-inhibited children to be able to work through their problem, they must experience the boundaries that parental discipline provides. Effective discipline places clear, but *not* harsh, limits on children's behavior. As children recognize that there are external limits, they begin to develop an internal sense of what it takes to be successful on their own, apart from their parents. They become self-disciplined. With inner control, children can develop the emotional maturity to adapt to the demands and the rules of the classroom and playground.

Positive Reinforcement for Appropriate Behaviors

Just as children need to hear from their parents about behaviors that are unacceptable, it is especially important for work-inhibited children to receive positive responses for appropriate social activity. Parents should notice and comment on behaviors that are friendly, cooperative, helpful, and courteous. It is unnecessary to give tangible rewards to children for pleasant behavior; rather, just a smile or a thank you is enough. This type of positive reinforcement has been found effective in shaping the behavior of children, while at the same time providing the nurturing that promotes self-esteem and caring parent-child relationships.

Promoting Autonomy/Independence

The goal of parenting is for children to grow gradually to productive independence. In the case of work-inhibited students, something has gone awry; these children are off course and their progress has been impeded.

Action must be taken to enable them to grow to self-sufficiency. Parents may help by showing ample affection, providing clear guidelines for what is expected, and then by giving the children plenty of freedom to be autonomous.

FREEDOM

From the time children begin crawling, they benefit from opportunities to explore their world apart from their parents. Such explorations enable them to grow in knowledge and to develop a sense of mastery that promotes self-confidence.

Unfortunately, it is not always easy for parents to encourage autonomy in their children. Anxiety and worry may inhibit parents from willingly backing away. From the earliest days in a child's life, parents worry about catastrophic events— putting a finger in a light socket, falling down stairs, being kidnapped or abused, falling into the wrong company, or being in an automobile accident. Parents who themselves lack self-confidence are especially prone to doubt that their children will be safe or will do well apart from them.

Separation is not easy. One mother recalled one morning decades ago when her two-year-old walked from their front steps to the neighbor's adjoining yard to play in the sandbox.

I just watched him go. He didn't seem to mind being on his own. He didn't need me to be right there. I watched through the door in case something might happen. It was a new experience for both of us. He had watched the older kids in the sandbox and just then, no one was there and he asked if he could go. All of a sudden I felt so sad, but at the same time triumphant that my little boy could be so easily apart from me.

Through the years those conflicting feelings returned to me as I saw Eric off to nursery school, then kindergarten, first grade, high school, and college. Always feeling triumphant for his confidence, sad about my loss, and frightened that something awful might happen.

I've spoken with other mothers and my feelings aren't unusual. I think my situation was made easier because Eric was not reckless, and he had such mature confidence. Otherwise, I might have had more difficulty encouraging and allowing him to be apart from me.

Not only parents have difficulty being separate. Children may also be reluctant to go it on their own, especially work-inhibited children. But no matter why children may have difficulty being separate, they need to be encouraged to get out there on their own.

GIVE UP INTRUSIVE BEHAVIORS

Parents can foster a sense of autonomy by simply not asking so many questions of their children. Parents who do not ask unnecessary questions, do not give too many reminders, and allow their children to be on their own support their children's growth toward independence.

How might a parent practice being unobtrusive and nonmeddling? First, unnecessary cautionary reminders should be avoided. A child is pouring milk. Parent says, "Be careful." Most "be carefuls" or "watch what you're doings" or "don't do thats" are said so often that they lose their impact. For some children, every venture may be coupled with an admonition. "Be careful." "Watch your step." "Look both ways." "Don't talk to strangers." "Don't spill your milk." "Don't do that."

These automatic reminders are often unnecessary and never

communicate confidence. Unless a situation is unusual or the child can really benefit from some information about how to proceed, parents should either say nothing or else give a positive message. "Enjoy your ice cream cone." "Have a good time. The Rebel Yell is a great roller coaster!" If something must be said, it should convey certainty, not a lack of confidence.

Show interest by being responsive to children's activities and comments. Be a good listener and do not demand that children reveal all that they do or think. Children like to share and may tell parents more if they feel that parents do not live or die with each success or failure.

Children also feel more comfortable and confident in their relationships with their parents when parents respect their right to privacy. Allow children to retreat to their rooms without barging in or knocking on the door and asking, "What are you doing?" Parents, too, should feel comfortable being apart from their children.

It is good for children to know their parents are interested in and supportive of their activities. But it is also good for children to see that their parents have interests and activities apart from their children's.

When parents enjoy pursuing their own interests, their work-inhibited children are more likely to break the bonds of infantile attachment. Parents of overly dependent children might look for opportunities to distance themselves from some of their children's activities. In today's culture, many extracurricular activities for children are supported and organized by adults. The value of such activities will be enhanced as parents give support and encouragement to children's participation, while also communicating that the activities belong to the children.

Some parents never miss seeing their children play in soccer, baseball, or basketball games, or other sports or cultural activities. It is as though organized sports for children were developed *not* to enable children to play, but rather to let them perform for an audience of adults who too often agonize over every goal, run, or basket.

Hooray for parents who encourage their children to play games for the child's own satisfaction! Hooray for fathers and mothers who occasionally are unable to watch their children's games because they have one of their own! It is useful for children to know that their parents have many of their own interests, and that it is all right to be apart.

TAKE DELIGHT IN NEW ADVENTURES

What an adventure growing up can be! At each stage of development, children have new worlds to explore, new responsibilities and challenges. It is not always easy, but it can be exciting! Many parents vividly recall their children's milestone accomplishments: swimming in the deep end of the pool, going off to kindergarten, learning to ride a bike, getting a driver's license, taking a trip with a friend, flying in an airplane alone, the first date, taking the subway into the city without parents, going to play alone in a neighbor's sandbox. How exciting!

It is best for parents to support their offspring's new ventures with confidence and joy. They should send children on their way with positive expectations that everything will be all right and that they will enjoy their new activities.

Parents should avoid hanging a dark cloud by communicating that life is dangerous and that failure is imminent. They should send children off with hugs and smiles. Children should be encouraged: "Take a chance." "Give it a try." "You can handle it." "Have a good trip." "Enjoy your new school." "Here's hoping you meet interesting people." "You are going to have an adventure." "Good luck on the job." "I know you will find your way, but if you need help, call me."

ALLOW CHILDREN TO MAKE MISTAKES

With encouragement, children are likely to try new ventures—and they will sometimes fail or make mistakes. What matters then is what children think about their mistakes. Since the consequences of most mistakes are small, children should not be taught to interpret their mistakes as global reflections of their worthlessness. Rather, they should be encouraged to view mistakes as an inevitable, natural part of learning and growing—something that everyone experiences.

As children grow up, it is good for them to see their parents struggle to complete tasks and make mistakes. Dad, in the kitchen making Sunday breakfast for the family, drops the buttered toast on the floor. He looks at the toast and then at the kids and says wryly, "Why is it that buttered toast always falls butter-side down?" The familiar lament puts the problem or mistake in perspective with humor, while Dad wipes up the mess and goes on with breakfast.

Parents should not exaggerate or make too much of mistakes, nor hide them from children. "Mom, can you take me to Beth's house?" "In a little while. I'm trying to balance the checkbook. I made a mistake somewhere and I'm trying to find it."

No one is perfect. Errors are part of everyone's daily experience. Parents' acceptance of their own imperfections reduces the likelihood that children will view their own struggles as overwhelming. "Mom and Dad do okay, and they're not perfect!"

Kids should be taught to make amends for their own mistakes. Twelve-year-old Jeff has decided to earn some money by mowing neighbors' lawns. Trina has decided to take on a paper route. Both children's plans provide good opportunities for their parents to promote independence. If they fail to do a good job or to complete tasks on time, they should learn to handle the inevitable complaints and learn to set things right with their customers. They should be in charge of their own successes and their own difficulties without Mom or Dad telling them, "Don't forget, Jeff, you have to mow Mr. Desmond's lawn," or "Trina, don't forget to do your collection."

It may be hard for parents to remain silent when their children make mistakes, but it is important to refrain from stating the obvious. Children know only too well the errors they commit while playing baseball or the missteps in the gymnastics routine.

While most mistakes should be ignored or given scant acknowledgement, there are times when parental intervention may be useful. Children need to know what their responsibilities are to others. When they break a window playing ball or lose something that belongs to a friend, they should make amends. Require them to replace or return the item. Accidents happen, mistakes are inevitable, but that does not lessen responsibility for individual behavior.

ALLOWANCE AND SPENDING

Giving children money on a scheduled, predictable, and agreed-upon basis is a useful tool in promoting independence. The best advice is that children be permitted to use their allowances pretty much as they wish. As long as they do not use money in a detrimental way, allow them to spend and save money as they please. It is possible for them to learn the benefits of saving for some prize that otherwise would not be available to them. Parents may model how to use money to advantage. But if children are to be given money, allow them to be masters of their finances.

Managing an allowance helps children feel positive about their ability to take care of themselves. As children get older, they may use their allowance and other money to make personal decisions about how they wish to express themselves. Encourage children to pick out their own clothes, to decorate their own rooms, and to choose their own activities.

Children benefit from having choices, but this does not mean they should have no limits. If a child needs new clothes for fall, provide a budget to stay within and encourage decision-making appropriate to the age. For a young child, the choice may be between a red coat and a blue. A teenager may shop alone or with friends. Children grow in independence when parents permit them to make decisions appropriate for their age.

Parents of work-inhibited children should treat them in ways that promote their growth toward self-sufficiency. If children have positive relationships with their parents and are encouraged to be individuals, while living within clear boundaries, they are more likely to develop the emotional strength to handle their school responsibilities.

Parents as Teachers

Children love to learn. They may not want to learn what their teachers and parents want to teach them, but they do want to explore, acquire new skills, and find out more about what is interesting to them. Some children may not do the work of school, but that does not mean they do not want to learn. Parents of work-inhibited students need to do all they can to help their children experience the pleasures of learning.

One of the many joys of parenting is to observe and participate in the learning activities of children. Parents have a profound effect on children's early development of self-help skills, language, and a vast amount of information. After their children enter school, parents continue to play an important role in promoting their children's learning.

What should parents of work-inhibited students do and not do to promote their children's academic growth? First, they should be involved with their children's learning activities by finding the "teachable moment" to encourage, reinforce, or assist. The teachable moment occurs when the child and parent are both interested and ready, perhaps when the child asks a question or when parent and child are engaged in an activity that enables the child to learn. Parents are not bound by the constrictions placed upon classroom teachers. They may go beyond the classroom, encouraging learning without having to evaluate and point out errors. It can be a no-risk situation.

School teachers organize learning activities to accommodate groups of twenty or more. They must adhere to schedules and follow specified curricula. Activities are not necessarily presented according to the interests of individual children. Workbooks, drills, and exercise sheets are used. Parents of work-inhibited children should not buy workbooks or invest in drill sheets or flash cards. It is unwise for parents to replicate at home what does not work at school. Instead, parents should just *be with the child,* participating in the fun of activities at home. When children ask questions or show an interest in knowing, be responsive to their initiatives. It is not necessary for parents to use the techniques employed by classroom teachers, since parents have no required curriculum and their relationship is often one-on-one.

Anything may serve as a learning experience. Working in the kitchen to prepare a meal provides opportunities to learn about weights, measures, and fractions—and cooperation. Watching television provides stimuli for discussion. Books and newspapers are sources for discovery. Trips provide opportunities for learning geography and map reading. Excursions to the zoo, museums, shopping malls, supermarkets, fairs, the city or the country provide opportunities for children to enrich their awareness and knowledge.

No at-home learning activity is recommended more frequently than reading. By and large, children love to be read to. Great benefits are derived from a parent reading something of interest to the child, the two snuggled together. It is a perfect pairing of emotional attachment and learning.

In many ways, parents as teachers have all the advantages. They can teach what they want, when the moment is appropriate—when the child is interested—and just for the joy of it.

Teaching by parents should not be lecture-based; the best

form is responsive dialogue. When children ask questions, give the answers they request. A common complaint of children is that parents give too much information. A child who asks what countries made up the Axis does not want a lecture on World War II! If a parent does not know an answer, together parent and child may seek out the answer from reference books in the home or in the library.

It is important for parents to avoid intrusive or scolding behaviors with work-inhibited children. When children are not in the mood, back away and look for the moment when they are interested about an issue or idea of their own. Work-inhibited children have erected emotional barriers to education and, in response to demands by adults, these barriers become more impenetrable. Allow children to lower their guard. When they do want help, are interested in going to see an exhibit, or want to know how to make chocolate chip cookies, join in with them.

Household Chores

Parents of work-inhibited children typically report that not only do their children not do their schoolwork, they also resist performing household chores. It is important for parents to require their children to complete household chores, since their continuous and successful completion enhances children's feelings of competence and self-esteem—however much they may complain about it. Of course, completion of household chores may also improve social behaviors outside the home and will certainly lessen work burdens on other members of the family.

What should parents do to help their children complete household chores? Be very clear about what chores are to be completed and when. Select chores that are appropriate to the individual characteristics of the child. Positive reinforcement for jobs well done and consequences for not completing chores should be part of the plan. It is also useful for parents to work with their children in the completion of some tasks.

Consider a nine-year-old who has never been able to complete household chores consistently. First, determine what chores are easily within the child's capability and do not require parental supervision. Select chores that the child is not overly averse to doing. Indeed, if possible, choose chores he or she may actually enjoy. After considering the possibilities, make a list of approximately five. Ask the child to choose which two or three he or she wants to do. Specify exactly how and when the task is to be completed.

Household chores may be put in writing and posted in some obvious place—perhaps on the refrigerator. Parents may then check to see if the task is completed and check it off or else have the child do so. If the task is not completed, it is important for the parent *not to nag*. Instead, the child may be prohibited from engaging in some pleasurable behavior such as watching television or going out to play. Quiet, consistent insistence by the parent is very helpful. The follow-through not only helps children meet their responsibility, it also fosters the growth of good work habits and autonomy.

This all sounds easier than it usually is! So parents, be smart! When trying to turn around a reluctant worker, begin with easy tasks that require little effort and that are likely to be completed. Modest success is always better than failure.

When children complete tasks, give appropriate positive feedback: "Thanks, I appreciate the help. The lawn really looks nice." Genuine smiles and statements of appreciation go a long way. Do not respond to task completion with comments about the total worth of the child: "You're such a wonderful boy!" "I'm so proud to have you as my daughter!" Also avoid overstatements: "What a wonderful job! I can't imagine anyone doing a better job!"

While it is valuable for children to have individual responsibilities, it is also good to share jobs with them. From time to time the whole family may work together to rake the leaves, clean the basement, or paint the house. Other chores may be not so large, but the child may be reluctant to do it on his or her own. A parent may say, "Let's clean your room together!" or everyone in the family may participate in the ritual of clearing the table and doing the dishes.

Parents frequently wonder whether they should pay their children for the jobs they complete. This practice may produce negative outcomes. Children may think they are working for their parents rather than engaging in cooperative efforts for the benefit of all members of the household. Parents may find their children want to negotiate payment in response to a simple request for help. Instead of paying children for jobs, give an allowance that is not tied to performance. It is just a given. The payoffs to children for doing their work are positive reinforcement from parents, a sense of accomplishment, and a growth in self-esteem.

Homework

Beginning with kindergarten and first grade, it is useful to let children know that schoolwork is *their* responsibility. Children who become successful students are able to do their own assignments independently, seek help as needed, and take charge of what they see as their responsibility. The task for parents is to nurture their children toward this academic self-sufficiency.

It is easy for parents of work-inhibited students to become overly involved in their children's homework. They fear that continued poor work habits will doom their children to a lifetime of unfulfilled promise. These parents want to do all they can to help, so they develop schemes to ensure that homework is completed. Too often the product of their interventions is a student who becomes more dependent, insecure, and angry.

It is not easy for parents of work-inhibited students to help their children complete homework assignments, while at the same time promoting independence and maintaining harmony at home. The problem may be further complicated by messages sent from school telling parents that they should be closely involved in their children's school life and ensure that daily assignments are completed. U.S. Department of Education publications *A Nation at Risk* and *What Works* both emphasize the importance of parental involvement and homework as principal determinants of children's and the nation's growth toward success.

But advice for parents seems to be contradictory. On one hand, the experts say, "Be involved." On the other, they say, "Allow the child to do his work on his own." Parents of work-inhibited students have a special mandate to help without being demanding, angry, or punitive.

Each family and child is different and no one set of specific recommendations applies to all. But there are some practices that clearly must be avoided and others that should be followed. The suggestions are not designed to ensure that work-inhibited students quickly become proficient in doing schoolwork. Rather, they aid children in their struggle toward self-sufficiency, not only in completing school assignments, but also in improving relationships with their parents and improving their own mental health.

One ninth-grader was asked, "You know kids who always do their schoolwork and kids who hardly ever do their class and homework assignments. What's the difference between the parents of the kids who do their work and the parents of those who don't?"

Without hesitation, the student replied, "Oh, that's easy! The parents of the kids who do their work *never* tell them to do it, and the parents of the kids who don't do their work *always* tell them."

Just as frequent reminders to do household chores are generally ineffective in getting children to complete those tasks, they are also ineffective in improving work-inhibited students' proficiency in completing their assigned homework. Rather than continuing unproductive nagging and inquisitions, parents may be more effective if they tell their children simply and directly that schoolwork is their own responsibility.

Parents must recognize that if a child does not want to do homework, the child holds the trump card. Parents cannot make the child be independently persistent. It really is up to the child.

But the parent *can* be helpful and *can* set the stage for improving the odds for success. To begin, it is helpful for parents to learn from their child's teachers what role homework plays in the educational program. In the early grades, the average student may be expected to complete thirty minutes of homework a night. By the fourth grade, teachers may expect up to an hour. The burden of homework grows through high school, when a reasonably conscientious student may average two hours or more of homework per day.

With a sense of how much time to estimate for assignments, parents may discuss with their children expectations of how much after-school time to reserve for the completion of homework. Set a specific time each day for a regular at-home study period. The period of time need not be the same each day and it may be right after school or in the evening. Indeed, some children may do their homework early in the morning before going to school. But no matter what part of the day or for how long, this period should be a quiet time. Parents can establish a positive environment by seeing that the television and stereo are not playing and that telephone conversation is postponed.

Parents cannot *make* their children learn and study, but they can *encourage, offer assistance, and establish certain basic requirements*. Parents may communicate gently and clearly to their children that they are there to help. They can provide their children with an atmosphere that is conducive to study, with the stated offer, "If you need help, please ask."

While most children do not like homework, work-inhibited students *hate* it. These children routinely spend three hours in restless distress, pondering the desperation of their situation. And then they will sometimes complete the assignment in fifteen minutes.

Parents should minimize the awfulness of homework. This might be accomplished in part by helping children restrict their after-school work time to the predetermined schedule. In this way, a child knows that after the quiet/study time is up, it is possible to pursue other activities.

It is useful for work-inhibited children to know that if a problem is hard or something is confusing, they may go to Mom or Dad for help. For that matter, they may obtain help from siblings or friends. Children should be encouraged to ask for help. When asked, parents should do their best to give the answer, practice the spelling words, do the math drill, and give any assistance that will make it easier for the child. A first step to improvement for work-inhibited children occurs when they begin to seek assistance.

Parents should not critique or correct homework unless asked. Work-inhibited children have such weak self-esteem that they do not handle criticism well. Many parents want to be helpful, so each night they insist on reviewing the work of their children. This intrusive ritual often makes a child want to keep as much information from parents as possible.

As children enter secondary school, with its more advanced concepts, parents typically do not possess the knowledge to give assistance in all courses. If their children are struggling, others may be enlisted to help. Encourage the student to get together with a classmate to work through assignments. In some instances a tutor may be employed or an older sibling be asked to help. Do not force such assistance on children. Rather, offer the suggestion and see if there is interest.

A common problem for parents of work-inhibited students is what to do when the teacher calls and says:

Mrs. Hoffman, I'm calling about Mike's classwork and homework. He is just not doing it. During the past six weeks, he has turned in only three of fifteen homework assignments, and he rarely works in class. I want you to know he is no problem to others. He's polite, and he gets along with the other students. I know this problem is not a new one for Mike. I just thought you should know that if he doesn't have a turnaround, he is going to fail the quarter.

What does Mrs. Hoffman do with this bad news? One action is to meet with school staff to find the means to help Mike at school. But Mrs. Hoffman also needs to communicate the teacher's message to her son, using a simple, straightforward approach.

Mike, your teacher called today and said. . . . It sounds as though everything is not going well for you. Perhaps I can help. Is there anything I can do to make it easier for you to do your work?

One difficulty with teachers' calls to parents is that teachers often describe the problem, but then do not offer a plan of action. The implication quite often is, "Parents, *you* fix the problem." But parents should resist the feelings of anxiety that arise naturally from being called on the carpet by the teacher. Keep as calm as possible, and follow the suggestions in this chapter.

COMMUNICATION WITH EDUCATORS

Let teachers know that although you do not blame them for your child's work inhibition and that you do not feel it is their fault, their help is needed nevertheless to turn the problem around. Teachers who feel personally responsible for a child's work inhibition may be more prone to be defensive or angry and may perhaps reject the student in greatest need of empathetic support. Teachers respond most positively to those students who comply with their requests. And any child who persistently fails to do assignments automatically invites rejection.

Participate in conferences with teachers. Engage the help of other school professionals. A teacher who has the support of the principal, guidance counselor, and school psychologist —all of whom should help the teacher understand that work inhibition occurs in children with poor self-esteem—is more likely to follow the suggestions offered to teachers in Chapter 6.

One strategy that all parents should employ is to ask the school for help. Paint a picture of a child troubled by his or her own sense of inadequacy, who is dependent and fearful of failure. Ask teachers not to ignore, reject, or punish your child. Work-inhibited children have the best chance to grow out of their insufficiency when parents and teachers pull together in a positive direction.

IN PERSPECTIVE

Put the problem of academic or work inhibition in perspective. A child who muddles through school with the nurturing, yet not intrusive, support of his or her parents may have a better chance of success in life than another child who experiences parental rejection and hostility. Work-inhibited children who enjoy good relationships with their parents are likely to find their own way.

Parents should not have to face the problems of work inhibition alone. This is an educational problem and school counselors are available to help; their assistance should be sought. When family relationships require intervention for improvement, a psychotherapist should be asked to help. Counselors and psychotherapists can play significant roles in work inhibition, which are described in Chapter 8.

8 / Counseling for Work-Inhibited Students

For work-inhibited students, sitting down and doing schoolwork is painful. It simply is the worst part of their life. They hate it.

The situation would be bad enough in itself, but it's really worse than that. Their parents, their teachers, and often their friends let them know—in no uncertain terms—that doing well in school is the most important job of all.

If they don't do well, they're "screw-ups," "real goof balls." And in the face of all this humiliation, parents and teachers let them know that they could do it, if only they wanted to, while the other students just think they're stupid.

Work-inhibited students do not always express their discomfort verbally. But it is not hard to recognize their distress as they fumble, avoid, sigh, and grimace while simply attempting to copy sentences and insert the missing punctuation.

While helping students overcome work inhibition is not easy, the best hope exists when parents, teachers, and other school personnel support and practice the effective techniques detailed in Chapters 6 and 7. Besides educators and parents, however, a third player is needed for success: the mental health professional.

Counselors within school systems and psychotherapists in the community possess the knowledge and skills to assist students, parents, and teachers. These professionals can help reduce the tremendous pain associated with inability to do the work of school. Counselors and psychotherapists can help teachers and parents develop the skills necessary to assist work-inhibited students. They also can help students overcome barriers to success, frustration, and pain, helping them grow to greater self-sufficiency.

This chapter discusses the roles that school counselors and psychotherapists play in dealing with work inhibition. In the schools, counselors may include school psychologists as well as guidance counselors. Psychotherapists may include clinical psychologists (usually Ph.D.'s), psychiatrists, counselors, and social workers.

Parents and teachers may also gain insight from this chapter concerning the kind of help they can seek from these mental health professionals. What follows are specific suggestions for counseling with young children, counseling and consulting with parents and teachers of students of all ages, the particular difficulties associated with the transition from elementary to secondary school, counseling with teens, and, finally, getting help from psychotherapists.

School Counselors

No group of professionals is in a better position to help work-inhibited students than school counselors. Unlike psychotherapists, school counselors work right where the problem is played out, so they can initiate action when they recognize a problem. They can go into classrooms to observe, offer help to teachers, and bring parents in for consultations. They can counsel teachers and students individually in their offices. School counselors can organize support systems both within and outside the school walls. They can collaborate with psychotherapists to develop appropriate treatment plans and to ensure that treatment goals are supported.

This chapter speaks to all school counselors, with special guidelines for the various educational levels. While the activities of counselors at the senior-high level differ from those at the elementary school level, there are three guiding principles for counseling work-inhibited students at all grade levels.

1. Pair comfort with work. Counseling serves as a model for what work-inhibited students should experience at home and school, i.e., work paired with acceptance and warmth.
2. Provide empathetic interpretations of the child's experiences in school and at home. Communicate this information to parents and teachers.
3. Propose plan(s) of action to parents, teachers, and students. "If we do this, then that is likely to happen."

How counselors in elementary through senior high school carry out these principles is the main theme of this chapter.

COUNSELING IN THE ELEMENTARY SCHOOLS

How does counseling at the elementary school level work? It is unlikely that an eight- or nine-year-old child would be sophisticated enough to schedule an appointment concerning his or her problems doing schoolwork. Unfortunately, it is similarly uncommon for older children to seek assistance for this problem. Instead, counselors at all levels must reach out to work-inhibited students. First, of course, these students must be identified (see Chapter 5). Once identified, though, what specific counseling techniques might be employed to help the young work-inhibited student?

ACTIVITY-ORIENTED COUNSELING: PAIR WORK WITH COMFORT

Counseling with young children proceeds most effectively through the use of structured activities. Children are more likely to learn to work when work is paired with comfort (i.e., support and encouragement) and as they develop a sense of their own competence—that they *can* do the work.

One effective method is for the counselor to ask work-inhibited students to bring to the counseling room assignments that they typically do not complete. Alternatively, the counselor may request that the teacher provide specific assignments for the child to bring to the counseling session. In either case, the counselor will have in hand one or more classroom assignments to be completed by the student.

Counselors might begin by telling the child:

> I'm going to spend some time with you while you work on some of your assignments. Your teacher is concerned about your progress in getting your work done. She thinks this is something that concerns you, too. I want to see if I can help. Show me what you have to do with this assignment and what difficulties you're having. Can you tell me about it?

Work-inhibited children's responses will vary. Some students will be highly cooperative and attentive, and will speak up readily regarding the assignment. They may even take the counselor's suggestion to give a try at doing the work.

Others may be very quiet, offering the counselor little feedback. They may not be willing to give the exercise even an attempt.

Depending on the child's response, counselors may say, "Go ahead and work on this. While you are working, talk out loud about how you're solving the problem or what you're thinking."

Children should be permitted—and encouraged—to say anything. What is important is for the counselor to *listen* and *not* to deny whatever feelings the child expresses.

Children who hate math, for example, may say, "This is stupid." As children talk about their displeasure or demonstrate their resistance by not working with the counselor no matter what, behaviors are presented that offer opportunities for counselors to understand what makes the children tick.

Eventually, the children themselves may begin to understand their own feelings, and why they behave as they do.

In these sessions, counselors can offer to help the children work. They can say, "Tell me about this. What has to be done?" "Is this difficult to understand?" "How about if I do the first one?"

The sessions should proceed with the counselor sitting next to the child—encouraging the child to think aloud about what is going on in his or her mind during problem-solving, spelling practice, looking for punctuation errors, or writing sentences or paragraphs.

From time to time, the counselor might reflect back to the child what is happening. Counselors are cautioned to limit their comments as the child describes problem-solving strategies or feelings. When children feel their thoughts are accepted, they are likely to be more willing to speak and more likely to feel accepted themselves.

After a session or two, a routine or schedule is developed. For example, the child may have a weekly or biweekly appointment with the counselor. The child might spend about half the typical thirty-minute counseling session doing school assignments and thinking aloud, while the counselor provides verbal and nonverbal acceptance.

During this first half of the session, the counselor *listens* and *interprets* for the child what is happening. When the counselor does not know what to say—no problem. The counselor should say nothing. The quiet acceptance of the child working or not working effectively is an important tonic.

What to say? What to interpret? Counselors should just play back to the child what they perceive is happening or what the child is saying. "Your frown tells me you're feeling tense." "You think it's not okay to make a mistake." "That was quick." "You get nervous when your teacher yells." "It looks as though you are confused." "You're smiling."

As the child works during the first part of the session, he

or she may need considerable assistance to do anything at all. Other students may find it easy to work with the counselor sitting next to them. No matter what is or is not accomplished during the first half, the work is put aside.

At the midpoint of the session, the activity changes. At this time, the child should choose from a variety of offerings: drawing, playing a card game, building a model, playing a board game, or maybe just talking. The child takes the initiative, while the counselor participates as the activity dictates.

Play is important. Through play, counselors enhance their relationship with the student and provide another opportunity for children to express themselves.

What does the child gain from these experiences with the counselor? Over time, the work-inhibited child is likely to discover a greater sense of competency, a feeling that "I can do this work." The child will experience an increased sense of acceptance: "My counselor likes me." This combination of doing well and having feelings of acceptance will enhance the child's self-esteem.

SOCIAL COMPONENT OF COUNSELING

Children's classroom experiences are composed of much more than listening and responding to their teachers and doing their work. At all levels, classrooms are the setting for complex social interactions in which some work-inhibited students fare poorly in their relationships with peers as well as in their work.

These children may be passive and have difficulty taking charge of their social life. Dependent and insecure, they may find it difficult to join in and to assert themselves. Such children are likely to be more comfortable right next to their teacher than joining in the unstructured games of childhood.

Some work-inhibited students are passive-aggressive. They are angry, but are unaware of their angry feelings. They manifest anger in indirect, subversive ways (see Chapter 3). These passive-aggressive children are likely to join in the activities of school social life, but they often alienate their peers and teachers when they indirectly disrupt activities.

For the counselor, the challenge is to help socially under-developed children to improve their social prowess as well as their work skills. Work-inhibited students are best able to grow to independence when they feel positively affiliated, or connected, and comfortable in their work environment. Whenever work-inhibited students possess poor peer relationships, it is important for them to acquire the necessary skills to enter social activities without inviting rejection.

Using work and play activities, counselors can help children recognize and identify the feelings they express. In the counseling setting, children can learn to express anger safely as they break up a stack of blocks or draw scary pictures. When children express themselves, counselors can help them identify their feelings: "Do you know that being scared is a feeling?"

As children become more comfortable with their own "bad" feelings and begin to recognize that everyone feels angry or sad at times, they begin to feel less frightened, less worried, and more accepting of themselves. Self-acceptance sets the stage for improved self-esteem. The acceptance of their counselors enables work-inhibited children to build trusting relations with others. With this insight and acceptance, children begin to develop a sense of mastery of their feelings. They may become more able to express their worries and anger in positive, rather than maladaptive, ways. Children may become more assertive and less passive or passive-aggressive.

GROUP COUNSELING

While counselors often work with one child at a time, group activities may offer an effective means of helping students improve their social skills. Using a variety of structured play activities, counselors can use group counseling (two to four students) to teach cooperation, an important element of social interaction.

All children (especially work-inhibited children) are self-centered, having difficulty understanding other people's feelings and points of view. Structured play activities give counselors opportunities to teach children basic social rules for give-and-take. "It's your turn, Johnny. You start." "What happens when Sally holds the dice?" This approach provides an opportunity for children to interpret what effect their behavior has on others.

Group counseling may take many forms. For example, consider Brendon, a third-grader who not only was work-inhibited, but who also seemed to have no real friends. Brendon wanted a chum. In this case, the counselor found another third-grader, Steven, who shared some of Brendon's problems—difficulty finishing work and interacting socially. The counselor arranged to see the boys together. Brendon and Steven spent the counseling sessions discussing and doing some of their schoolwork and playing various games.

The counselor had several goals for Brendon and Steven: to help the boys improve their social skills, to give them a sense of increased affiliation by providing an important social opportunity (perhaps they might even become friends), to help them identify their own sense of self, and to help them learn to be better workers.

Group counseling helps children improve their social skills, shows them that they are not the only ones with problems, and enables counselors to see more children.

REFLECTIVE LISTENING

For children who are failing in their schoolwork and/or their social life, counseling often makes a real contribution to improving their quality of life. Positive outcomes are most likely to occur when counselors follow the three important rules for counseling: listen, listen, listen.

Perhaps the greatest deterrent to effective counseling is preaching by the professional. In counseling sessions, children are likely to reveal ideas and feelings that may tempt counselors to correct the child's message. "I hate my brother." "My Dad's mean." "Sometimes I wish my sister was never born." "I'd like to burn this place down."

While it is not surprising that many adults might say, "You really don't mean that," the professional counselor knows better. In the counseling environment, children must have the freedom to express themselves. Counseling enables children to realize that acknowledging and expressing their true feelings and thoughts will not jeopardize their relationship with their counselor, that angry feelings do not make them evil. They may even begin to find more effective ways to communicate their feelings.

Attentive, reflective listening to work-inhibited children's concerns fosters trust. With acceptance by the counselor, it becomes possible for children to accept themselves and to overcome feelings of inadequacy. Furthermore, with improved social skills, children feel more empowered. They will become increasingly ready to develop solutions to problems as they are worked out in the counseling sessions.

COUNSELING:
CONSULTING WITH PARENTS AND TEACHERS

Through work-and-play sessions, counselors identify children's individual characteristics. Knowing children's individual skills, abilities, temperaments, likes, dislikes, and perceptions of self and others, counselors identify the environmental factors at home and in the classroom that impede or enhance academic performance. Through patient and attentive counseling activities, counselors become experts; they really come to know their clients. Armed with their knowledge, they can develop a coherent plan for parents and teachers and give them examples of specific techniques.

"I've noticed that Todd does better when he is given repeated feedback that his efforts are on target and that he is progressing nicely."

Parents and teachers need help in learning how to respond effectively to work-inhibited students. What happens between counselors and students should be a model for teachers and students, as well as parents and their children. In essence, counselors help parents and teachers pair comfort with work —to be accepting and nurturing, to empower children to make decisions on their own and to take positive actions. (A note of caution: effective and ethical practice does not permit counselors to break trusts—to share information given in confidence.)

Counseling, then, should not merely be an interaction between child and counselor. Teachers and parents are also clients of the school counselor. As is true for children, teachers and parents also need to be listened to carefully.

It is critical to invite parents to consult with the counselor. Rather than immediately offering assessments of the problem, it may be more productive for the counselor to ask parents to relate how they see their children and their problems.

Most parents enjoy talking about what is most precious to them—their children. Parents are much more likely to feel comfortable and ready to join in with the school when they feel invited and when they feel their input is valued.

After listening, counselors should ask parents what they would like the school to do for their children. Parents, too, must feel empowered in order to have a sense of control and participation.

Counselors should then share with parents their impressions of the counseling process. This information will help teachers, parents, and counselors decide together what courses of action to take at home and at school.

It is common for parents and teachers of work-inhibited students to feel both angry and insecure about this problem. Parents want desperately for their children to do well, and when they just don't—when they seem so incapable of putting forth effort—it stands to reason that parents become angry and demand that these children change their behaviors and attitudes.

Within the classroom, after months of unsuccessful efforts, teachers may also become frustrated. Teachers often feel as though *they* are the failures. They think that if they did a better job, the students would do their work.

Counselors can provide a valuable service to teachers and parents by bringing them together. As the problems and positive attributes of the child are considered together—and as all parties feel more positive about the common purpose of helping the child—the counselor may begin to propose solutions.

In counseling and consulting with parents and teachers, counselors have the opportunity to pair insights about individual students with what they know about work-inhibited students in general. With this knowledge, they can engineer a plan of action to benefit specific children. Counselors should aim to:

- Help both parents and teachers understand the dynamics of work inhibition. Work-inhibited students must not be dismissed as lazy. Work inhibition must be seen as a symptom of poor self-esteem and dependency.
- Identify children's specific strengths and weaknesses. Exploit students' strengths—public speaking, swimming, computers, skateboarding, or whatever. Emphasize, encourage, and allow children to engage in activities about which they feel happy and positive, while providing support and comfort to students while they do school assignments.
- Identify what is and what is not the problem. Avoid getting sidetracked by issues that are not relevant; keep parents and teachers concentrated on the present problem.

For example, "Adrian's fourth-grade teacher may or may not have been effective. What happened two years ago is not the concern here today. What we need to determine is what work Adrian is having difficulty completing."

- Provide encouragement and support. Parents and teachers need pats on the back for their efforts.
- Develop a homework plan. It is very important that teachers encourage parents to take a supportive, but not directive, approach. See Chapter 7 for parent tips on dealing with homework.
- Develop a system of communication to ensure that all parties continue to discuss their problems. Get together to share successes and setbacks. Remind all concerned that even with the best course of action, it takes time for students to grow to self-sufficiency.

From time to time, counselors may need to remind parents and teachers of the importance of teamwork. "We have the best chance of solving this problem if we work together."

Bringing parents and teachers together is helpful during both elementary and secondary schools. At all grade levels, empathetic, knowledgeable, and reassuring counselors can be agents of dramatic change in their schools by helping work-inhibited students directly and by showing parents and teachers how to help these students work independently.

Transition from Elementary to High School and Why the Teen Years Can Be So Difficult for Work-Inhibited Students

During elementary school, children are expected to acquire knowledge and basic academic skills. They learn complex social behavior and they learn to work—practices that will enable them to become effective adults. Successful children develop pride in being self-sufficient.

When children fail to master their work lives during the elementary school years, this task then can become an even greater burden during adolescence. Already weighed down by problems in school, low self-esteem, and probably strained relations at home, these children often encounter more trouble in adolescence, when developmental separation from parents intensifies.

Teenagers look to their peers for images of what they want to be. At school they are expected to accomplish increasingly more complex tasks that require sustained effort. At the same time that psychological and social issues become more complex, teenagers experience rapid physical and sexual growth. It is no wonder that confusion and doubt are normal experiences at this time. And for work-inhibited students who enter adolescence without having mastered the early issues of autonomy, and who remain insecure, the teen years can be especially troublesome.

The first year of junior high or middle school can be scary, but it can also be exciting. For some children, this year is something like the "terrible twos." Suddenly, everything Mom and Dad say is wrong. Young teenagers may look away from their parents toward idealized adults (entertainers, star athletes, drama teachers, athletic coaches, etc.), but they mostly look to peers. During these years, teens are normally preoccupied with thoughts about how they appear to others of their age. They worry, "Am I normal?" "Do I look okay?" "I'm such a geek!"

These middle years between childhood and later adolescence are times of discovery. Young teens begin to experience rapid body growth and oncoming sexual maturity and eventually begin to fall in love. Whether they know it or not, teens also begin to discover who they are.

Adolescents are faced with so many demands—do what the teachers want, live up to parental expectations, dress with just the right degree of casualness (perhaps with the "right" labels), develop and nurture friendships, take care of home responsibilities, do well in sports or drama or in youth groups, do everything to ensure being well-liked. So much is expected, and yet these teenagers are also treated like children.

Successful teenagers work hard. They balance demands from teachers, parents, coaches, and employers with their own need to be affiliated with peers. Many adults look back at their years in junior and senior high school as a time when they learned independence, got the grades, and (one hopes) had fun. It was often the time when they were quick to point out the many hypocrisies that existed in their world.

For those students who enter adolescence without having experienced success in the independent completion of school assignments, the possibilities for future problems are high. Work-inhibited students are already dependent and insecure, and the added social, work, and emotional demands of this age put these students at risk for failure. Counselors must help these students avoid being overcome by their feelings of inadequacy and their fears that they will never amount to much.

In some respects, counseling teens is easier than counseling elementary school youth. In contrast with younger children, teenagers are better able to put their thoughts into words. They are able to describe events and they have begun to appreciate the thoughts and concerns of others. With help from their counselors, young teens learn to understand why their parents may be upset or why a certain teacher gets so "bent out of shape." As the years progress, teens develop the cognitive maturity to become increasingly introspective. With these added abilities, counseling can change from the concrete use of activities (as suggested for work with young, elementary-age students) and become dialogue-centered.

COUNSELING IN THE SECONDARY SCHOOLS

Earlier in this chapter, three guiding principles were presented for counseling work-inhibited students at all grade levels: pair work with comfort, interpret experiences, and provide solutions. Secondary school counselors have their work cut out for them when trying to help work-inhibited students feel affiliated and comfortable with their school. Counseling offers opportunities for work-inhibited students to learn about themselves and others; one hopes they can then discover ways to take charge of their own interests and responsibilities.

In order for work-inhibited teens to overcome their difficulties in sustaining effort, they must develop a sense of comfort with their school. Individual and group counseling can be a nurturing experience, enabling students to realize they are valued members of the school.

Most teens are able (though not always immediately willing) to express their interests and concerns. And teens really appreciate adults who listen. A central and often-repeated theme of this book is that relationships and trust can be developed between parents and children, between teachers and students, and between counselors and students simply by attentive, nonjudgmental listening. While young children's ideas and thoughts can be brought out through shared activities, it is often possible to initiate a flow of ideas with teens simply by inviting them to describe and reflect on what is of interest and concern to them.

Scheduled weekly counseling sessions will enable students to develop a healthy sense of importance. "Someone cares. I must be worthwhile."

Counseling may also enable the student to become introspective. "I worry too much." "I get so mad." "My parents are always on my case. I just feel as though they are never satisfied." "I would do all right if I didn't have homework." "I know they only want what's best for me." "I couldn't be a

teacher. They take so much crap. I wouldn't li[
with me."

A counselor's main task is to listen. He or sh
go along for the ride, while encouraging studen
thoughts about classes, school assignments, and
to consider their friends', parents', and teachers' points of view.
"What do you think your parents/teachers are thinking?"
"What do your friends have to say?" "Tell me more about these
feelings." "What do you think your parents will say when they
see your report card? And then what will you do?"

Students enjoy problem-solving and sharing with counselors
who they believe have a genuine interest in them and who are
their advocates. Even if all that is accomplished through counseling is the development of one positive relationship, counseling may be deemed worthwhile. The real breakthrough for
work-inhibited students occurs, however, when students become introspective, when they begin to identify and understand their own feelings.

One of the characteristics of work inhibition is that the
strong, overt emotions of anger, frustration, anxiety, and worry
are experienced by parents and teachers—while the work-
inhibited students appear, at least on the surface, to be passive
and emotionally indifferent. It seems that all the emotional
energy is being spent by the parents and teachers. Rather than
the child "owning" the feelings of insecurity and anger, these
feelings have been foisted unconsciously by the students on
their parents and teachers, who then act on the emotions by
reminding, nagging, yelling, and punishing.

When students begin to identify feelings as their own, they
realize that their difficulties have been a result of these feelings. They often realize that they have been afraid to try, for
fear that they may not do as well as they would like—or what
is expected of them. Withholding effort is their way of not
failing, of not making others upset. But, of course, just the
opposite occurs.

When work-inhibited teenagers become introspective, it's as though a light bulb clicks on. They gain insight. They begin to make plans for themselves. They begin to take charge of their own destiny. It becomes possible for them to accept help from teachers and counselors, to begin to accept themselves and to acknowledge their own strengths. "I'm a pretty nice guy." "I like history and photography." "I'd better find a way to get better grades if I want to get that diploma."

As students accept their own feelings—and begin to *want* to become successful and to do their schoolwork—counselors can then help students find the emotional strength to stay with and finish school assignments. In essence, students will really *want* help. They will begin to join study groups, to accept the assistance of a tutor, and to meet with teachers after school to get the extra help that has always been offered. Remember that such successes take time and are not necessarily realized in every counselor-student relationship.

Group counseling may also be of benefit for teens. Group sessions may be topical in nature and include such issues as self-esteem, career decision-making, children of divorced parents, and effective study skills. The possibilities are nearly endless. The point is that work-inhibited students benefit from hearing about others' interests, problems, ideas, and concerns. Knowing that their own problems are not unique is very reassuring.

Counselors should invite work-inhibited students to join groups related to their interests; they should not form groups exclusively for work-inhibited students. These students do not benefit from being singled out based on their weakness.

Another benefit of group counseling is that it promotes affiliation. As the participants listen to each other and provide mutual support and encouragement, students are likely to experience increased feelings of well-being and importance as well as closer attachments to the counselor and their peers.

Chapter 6 emphasizes the importance of promoting work-inhibited students' connection to school. In this regard, counselors have opportunities to help these students, who may be ready to give up or drop out, by getting them involved in an organization or an activity.

It is not unusual for athletic coaches to remark that their players get their best grades during the sport's season. Students usually work more effectively when they feel a sense of positive identity with their teachers and their school. Wearing a letter jacket, playing in the band, working on the newspaper, or belonging to a club all enhance feelings of "connectedness." Work-inhibited students—more than most—need reassurance that they are important and are included. This sense of belonging gives them comfort in their place of work.

COUNSELING PARENTS AND TEACHERS

Counselors also need to practice damage control vis-à-vis parenting styles. At any school level, one of the challenges of consultation with the parents of work-inhibited students is to convince them that it is *not beneficial* to make schoolwork the focus of their relationships. To the extent that parents can maintain loving, encouraging, supportive (and not directive) relationships with their children, the greater the possibility that students will shed their work inhibition.

It cannot be emphasized enough that children, especially older students, do not overcome work inhibition easily or quickly. Counselors provide a valuable service by emphasizing this fact of life to parents and teachers. Both parents and teachers need to know that their supportive efforts are not wasted, even when results do not appear quickly. They should be reminded that the encouragement and support will pay off eventually as their children feel less defeat, less anger, less disapproval, and a greater sense of belonging. As their perception of support from others increases, work-inhibited students acquire the emotional strength to stay on course.

Help from Psychotherapists

Many parents seek help from psychotherapists when their child doesn't do his or her schoolwork. Therapists who provide help to families report work inhibition to be a frequent reason for referral. But is it imperative for parents to seek help outside of school channels when their children are work-inhibited? When parents, teachers, and counselors work together to support and encourage work-inhibited children, psychotherapy for children and their parents is not likely to be required.

There are instances, however, when psychotherapy can be very useful. Psychotherapy should be considered when the problem has a significant negative impact on family life. When work inhibition becomes the focus of relationships between parents and their children, psychotherapy can offer valuable help. Through psychotherapy, parents and children can learn to understand each other better and thus interact in a less stressful, more natural manner.

The role of the psychotherapist parallels and overlaps that of the school counselor. Both professionals help interpret for their clients the issue of work inhibition and what to do about it. The psychotherapist enables parents and children to explore specific, deeply personal, and lifelong patterns of communication within the family.

The usefulness of psychotherapy is illustrated by the case of eleven-year-old Roland Lang and his parents. The Langs were aware that their communication with Roland (especially during the school year) was poor. The parents were worried and tense. Family relations were always strained. Both parents, especially the father, would get very frustrated with Roland's lack of effort. On the advice of a school psychologist, but with considerable trepidation, the Langs began therapy with a clinical psychologist.

After about six months of therapy for their son and themselves, the Langs related that the sessions had indeed been a valuable investment of their time, energy, and money. Both parents agreed that the therapy was not the ordeal they had thought it might be. In fact, as the sessions progressed, they began to look forward to the meetings. Although some of the emotions they explored were painful, both husband and wife found it reassuring to communicate with each other about the feelings that had made it difficult for them to respond to Roland as they wished they might have.

The Langs learned through their sessions with the psychologist that they were actually pretty good parents and that, in most respects, Roland was okay. They also learned a great deal about their own parenting styles and how their behaviors were an extension of their own childhood experiences.

Both parents wanted Roland to have the opportunities that were not available to them. Dad spoke about his own childhood.

I was always the dutiful son. I did just about everything that was expected of me—worked after school, didn't go away to college, stayed at home. Our family didn't have much money, and I always felt a little guilty about asking for it. I didn't have a bad childhood, but I want my son to have some of the advantages that weren't available to me.

My wife and I are hardworking and perhaps—no, without a doubt—a bit intense. We worry too much and try too hard.

Our counseling sessions enabled us to realize that we have a nice family, but we need to loosen up. We need to give our son some space. We need to have a good time.

Each family's background is different, and dysfunctions emerge in different patterns. But to bring about the best possible result in treating work inhibition, therapy should be a family matter. Not much progress is achieved without parental involvement. Through active participation, parents learn why their children have difficulty doing their schoolwork. They learn how to improve relationships with their children while helping them grow toward self-sufficiency.

OBSTACLES TO THERAPY

For some, psychotherapy is a sensitive issue in and of itself, fraught with all sorts of emotions. But it can be vital for setting families of work-inhibited students on a better course for success. What is it that interferes with parents seeking therapy, and what might hinder prospects for effective counseling? Potential obstacles may lie with the children, the parents, or the therapists themselves.

Work-inhibited children and teenagers may not be amenable to therapeutic relationships. Many work-inhibited students are passive-aggressive or emotionally guarded. They have difficulty getting in touch with and expressing their feelings and thoughts. Such children do not make easy or quick emotional gains.

Reluctance to enter into psychotherapy is not unusual in this culture and, for many, a stigma is attached to going to a therapist. For some parents, getting past this stigma is the main obstacle to obtaining help. Some parents experience feelings of shame or guilt about having a child with work inhibition. Others ascribe blame to others. "It's the school's fault. They should take care of it."

Other reasons for avoiding therapy include: "He doesn't need help. He's just lazy." "I don't have the time. There must be another answer." "Maybe she will grow out of it."

Financial considerations may also inhibit parents from seeking mental health assistance. Parents are advised to contact their local mental health center for information on how to obtain affordable psychotherapy.

Instead of dwelling on reasons to avoid psychotherapy, parents are encouraged to think: "Our child has a problem. We haven't found a way to help, nor are we happy about the school's efforts to make things better. We need some help. The teachers need help. Let's do something."

THERAPIST SELECTION

Once parents decide to seek assistance from a psychotherapist, it is essential to find a good match for the problem. Since work inhibition is a school problem, it may be useful to ask for a referral from a local school psychologist or counselor. They may know which psychologists, psychiatrists, counselors, or social workers have good reputations for working with families with work-inhibited children. Referrals from local mental health centers may be helpful as well.

Finding the right therapist is crucial. Although the issue of not doing schoolwork is common, many therapists do not understand the dynamics of the problem. Some may inappropriately diagnose the child as depressed or determine that the child has learning disabilities. Before beginning therapy, parents are encouraged to interview prospective therapists to determine to what extent they have helped others who have had similar problems. (See Chapter 5 for a discussion of what is and what is not work inhibition.)

After parents decide to see a psychotherapist, how do they tell their children? First of all, they should not discuss or negotiate with the child the option of going or not going for therapy. Parents should schedule the appointment and then tell the child—but not too far in advance. They should use a matter-of-fact approach. In response, some children may protest. Parents should listen and briefly explain that the decision has been made.

It may be helpful for parents to ask the therapist when the appointment is being made what they should tell the child about the reasons for therapy. After the first appointment, the therapist will help work out problems that relate to resistant children.

One major problem reported by many parents is that after

months of treatment with their children, "the therapist never gave any feedback. We never found out what we were supposed to do." Parents need the instructive help of therapists. It is critical that parents be part of the treatment plan.

Psychotherapists' effectiveness is curtailed severely if they work with work-inhibited students in isolation. Parents must be included. Parents should be sure to establish from the beginning that the family is the focus and that they need direction in setting the problem to rights. Some arrangement should be made for consultation with teachers or school counselors so that a team approach is maintained. The aims of therapy are more likely to be realized when therapists work with all those connected with the problem. Therapists must share their insights and recommendations with teachers, school counselors, and parents.

THE THERAPEUTIC APPROACH

Psychotherapists employ different techniques in their work. Some therapists prefer cognitive techniques, some are behaviorally oriented, and others use a client-centered approach. All these orientations are effective in the treatment of work inhibition. It is important that the therapist be flexible and use those techniques that are most relevant to the client's needs.

Three important rules pertain to treatment for work-inhibited students:

1. Little is accomplished without the participation of the parents. Parents must be part of the process.
2. Separate therapy sessions should be scheduled for children and parents. An essential goal of treatment for work inhibition is to help students overcome their sense of powerlessness and their dependency. These children have not become autonomous. Individual therapy sessions offer opportunities for these children, not only to identify

and accept their own feelings, but also to become appropriately assertive.

Separate sessions for parents enable them to explore the emotions they experience that hinder their family relationships. It is unlikely that parents can be candid in the presence of their children. Also, during these sessions, psychotherapists have opportunities to interpret what is happening for all parties and determine what the parents can do to improve the situation.

3. The therapist should provide consultative services to the school. Therapists can greatly enhance the gains their patients make by consulting with teachers and school counselors. By enabling teachers to understand these students better and by helping them alter their own negative attitudes and behaviors, opportunities for success with work-inhibited students are heightened.

With counselors and psychotherapists supporting the efforts of parents and teachers, these children—who can, but don't—will be able to break through the emotional shackles that bind them to school failure.

Appendices

Appendix A:
Demographic Studies

A series of studies was conducted in February and March 1985 to determine the incidence of work inhibition, the prevalence of work inhibition within selected groups, and characteristics of work-inhibited students. This research was conducted in stages, the first of which entailed identifying all students for whom the number of completed class and homework assignments was significantly smaller than for the majority of students. After the target population was identified, studies were conducted that revealed how these work-inhibited students compared on a variety of dimensions to the general population within their school.

COMMUNITY IN WHICH STUDIES WERE CONDUCTED
The subjects of this study resided in Falls Church, Virginia, a small (population 9,500) suburb of Washington, D.C. In general, residents of this city are white, middle-class, well-educated professionals.

The community's school system is considered by many to be excellent. A favorable ratio of teachers to pupils enables classes to be small, average scores on national standardized tests are high (in the 70th and 80th percentiles), almost all students are on grade level for reading skills, and less than 1 percent of all students drop out of school. The high quality of the school system was attested to by the United States Department of Education, which twice recognized Falls Church schools for excellence. In 1983 the junior/senior high school and in 1986 the elementary schools were cited among the best in the nation.

METHODOLOGY

To begin, a definition for "work-inhibited student" was developed. To be considered work-inhibited, a student must have possessed a history of not completing school assignments to a substantial degree in all academic subjects for at least two years. The intent was to exclude students who were experiencing a short-term problem, such as not completing work for one teacher or avoiding doing work in one subject ("I don't like math."). Since the definition included the two-year criterion, students below third grade were excluded from the study.

All teachers and counselors were asked to review the work histories of their students and to provide a list of those who submitted less work than typical students. Teachers then reviewed the names submitted to determine if the problem existed across academic disciplines, among all teachers, and for at least two years.

A review of report cards was also conducted. Report cards included teacher comments and ratings of students' ability to complete work and stay on task. Summaries of parent-teacher conferences were also evaluated, which verified or negated the existence of the problem. When teachers disagreed about a child's work inhibition, or the record did not provide a clear picture of the problem, the student was not identified as work-inhibited. The final list included the names of only those students for whom both teachers and counselors agreed that completion of class and homework assignments was substantively less than for the majority of students.

TABLE 1. Number of Work-Inhibited Students

Grade	Boys	Girls	Total	Percent
3	3	0	3	4
4	5	5	10	13
5	8	4	12	16
6	11	0	11	15
7	18	3	21	24
8	5	4	9	12
9	15	5	20	20
10	13	5	18	19
11	13	6	19	28
12	15	5	20	24
TOTALS	106	37	143	18%

RESULTS

Table 1 illustrates the incidence of work inhibition among the surveyed population of 795 students in grades three through twelve.

Analysis of the data in Table 1 revealed that the incidence of work inhibition among all students was considerable at grade four, with percentages somewhat higher at the secondary level. Approximately three of every four work-inhibited students were boys. Eighteen percent of the school system's total population from grades three through twelve was determined to be work-inhibited.

After having identified the work-inhibited students, additional information was evaluated to determine if there was anything unique about this group of 143 students that might help explain why they were work-inhibited. Information was obtained by an exhaustive search of student records.

ACADEMIC/INTELLECTUAL ABILITIES

At least one intelligence test score was available for more than 75 percent of the work-inhibited students—111 of the 143. The

TABLE 2. Distribution of Intelligence Scores
of Work-Inhibited Students

Standard Score Range	Number of Students
80–89	1
90–99	11
100–109	20
110–119	39
120–129	25
130+	15
TOTAL	111

scores used were from individually administered tests (either the Wechsler Intelligence Scale for Children or the Stanford-Binet Intelligence Scale) or from group-administered tests (Otis-Lennon Test of Mental Abilities or the Educational Ability Test). Scores were unavailable for students who had enrolled in the Falls Church system after group intelligence tests had been administered for their class.

Table 2 shows the distribution of ability scores for the 111 work-inhibited students. The data represent one score for each student. For those students for whom more than one group test score was available, a median or mean score was derived and noted.

All tests utilized standard scores with approximate means of 100 and a standard deviation of 15 or 16. A score of 100 was an average score. Scores that ranged from 90 to 110 were considered within the average range.

The distribution of intelligence scores was definitely skewed toward the upper end of the scale. Only one work-inhibited student scored below the average range. Thirty-one students, approximately 28 percent of the work-inhibited population, earned average scores on intelligence tests. Seventy-nine students, approximately 71 percent of the work-inhibited group, measured above-average to superior for intellectual abilities.

Scores above 120 were considered to be in the superior range—36 percent of the students obtained such scores. A score of 130 fell at approximately the 98th percentile on national norms—a very superior score. Almost 14 percent of the identified work-inhibited students in Falls Church had such abilities.

It was clear that, as a group, the measured cognitive abilities of these work-inhibited students was above average. Indeed, the mean (average) IQ score was 115.

How did this compare with other Falls Church students? In 1985, the Science Research Associates Educational Ability Test was administered to tenth-grade students. The mean or average score for the entire grade was 114. These tenth-grade pupils also received scores that were distributed toward the upper end of the scale.

The work-inhibited students' intellectual abilities compared favorably with a sample of the total school population. By and large, *most work-inhibited students not only had good cognitive abilities, but also demonstrated above-average to superior thinking skills.*

ACADEMIC SKILLS

Norm-referenced achievement test scores were available for most work-inhibited students; at least one score of this type was recorded for 129 of the 143 students. In those instances where more than one score existed, the most recent score was used. Falls Church Schools used the Science Research Associates Achievement Tests (SRA). The scores displayed in the frequency distribution in Table 3 are normal curve equivalent (NCE) scores. The mean, or 50th percentile point, for these scores is 50 and the standard deviation is 20.

The pattern of achievement test scores for the work-inhibited population was generally equivalent to that of the general school population. Approximately 75 percent of the students scored above the 50th percentile point. Relatively few students ob-

TABLE 3. Distribution of SRA Achievement Scores
of Work-Inhibited Students

Equivalent Score Range	# STUDENTS		
	Reading	Mathematics	Language Arts
1–10	–	–	–
11–20	–	2	3
21–30	2	5	2
31–40	10	13	11
41–50	19	18	29
51–60	34	28	27
61–70	30	25	23
71–80	15	16	19
81–90	14	10	9
91–99	5	8	1
TOTAL STUDENTS	129	125	124
MEAN	60.9	59.2	56.9

tained scores that fell below the average range. In general, students in this group earned slightly higher scores on reading tests than on the math and language arts tests.

Mean scores obtained by the work-inhibited population and those earned by the 1985 tenth-grade class were compared. The tenth-grade students' SRA achievement scores yielded mean NCE scores of 62 in reading, 69 in mathematics, and 58 in language arts. The distribution of scores for both the tenth-grade class as a whole and the work-inhibited population was skewed toward the upper end of the range.

These work-inhibited students had persistently resisted the completion of school assignments for years. Yet their achievement test scores were reasonably equivalent to their academic ability or IQ scores. SRA Achievement Test scores and the academic ability scores available for 111 work-inhibited students also were compared. Only twenty-six students had one or more reading, math, or language arts achievement score that fell significantly below the obtained intelligence score. Significance in this analysis was one standard deviation.

In this analysis of academic ability and achievement tests, work-inhibited students' scores looked very much like those of the entire Falls Church student population. Their academic abilities and skills fell across the range from low to high. It seemed logical to assume that more work-inhibited students would have had academic deficiencies than they appeared to have, but less than 25 percent had even one discrepant weakness relative to their predicted ability. Furthermore, very few (about 10 percent) had academic skills that fell below the average range. As with other students in Falls Church, work-inhibited students also had been successful in acquiring basic academic skills.

INCIDENCE OF WORK-INHIBITED STUDENTS
AMONG IDENTIFIED SPECIAL POPULATIONS

Questions were asked concerning work inhibition in special populations. To what extent were work-inhibited students identified as needing special/differentiated instruction? Were these students more likely to need extra help to improve their academic skills? Or was it possible that work-inhibited students tended to be more able than others and, in so being, more likely to be identified as gifted?

A review of the records revealed that 15 percent of the 143 work-inhibited students were enrolled or had been enrolled in a program for the learning-disabled or had received reading instruction through the Chapter I assistance program. This compared closely with 14 percent for the total school population. Moreover, in this study 8.4 percent of the 143 work-inhibited students were identified as gifted. In the total school system, 10 percent of all students enrolled were identified as gifted.

The incidence of work inhibition among the learning-disabled and the number of work-inhibited students enrolled in Chapter I remedial reading programs and gifted programs were very similar to the percentages found in the total school population.

DISRUPTIVE BEHAVIOR

Were work-inhibited students more likely to engage in misbehavior than other students? In order to answer this question, a study of discipline records was conducted. Falls Church school principals maintain files for students referred to them for infractions of the rules. Any student sent out of class for disruptive behavior is seen by the principal or an assistant and a record is made of the event, time, place, causal circumstances, and the consequences.

A search of the 1984–85 school year discipline records for both work-inhibited and other students revealed that of the 143 work-inhibited students, thirty-five students (nearly 25 percent) had at least one disciplinary referral for disruptive behavior that year. Approximately 10 percent of all students had one or more disciplinary referrals during that same year.

While the work-inhibited population was referred more than twice as often as the general population for disruptive behavior, two points must be considered. First, of all students referred for disciplinary infractions, very few were girls. Because most work-inhibited students are boys, this tends to skew the data. If the comparison had been made among male students only, the difference between the work-inhibited population and the entire student body would not have been as large. Second, the principals noted that in most instances, a single disciplinary referral was not reflective of either severe or chronic misbehavior, and that few work-inhibited students engaged in pronounced disruptive/oppositional behavior.

ABOUT THE FAMILIES

Upon enrolling a child in school, parents must provide information on a school entrance form. The form requests that parents list family members and their level of education, occupation, and marital status.

In an attempt to gauge the socioeconomic status of the families of work-inhibited children, a study of mothers' level of education was explored. Data on mothers rather than fathers were chosen because there was more information provided on mothers. In this group of 119 mothers, only two mothers had not completed high school and at least fifty-nine had attended college.

From the school entrance form, it was also possible to determine which students lived with both natural parents and which children lived in other family configurations. Forty-one percent lived with both natural parents, another 41 percent lived in single-parent homes, and 15 percent lived with one parent and one step-parent (a blended family). In order to compare this distribution with the total population, a study was made of all sixth- and ninth-grade students. The survey revealed that in this two-grade sample, 59 percent of all students lived with both parents, 28 percent lived in single-parent homes, and 13 percent lived in blended families.

The order of birth was obtained for 141 of the 143 students. Thirty-three were found to be only children, thirty-eight were oldest, twenty-six were middle, and forty-four were youngest children. Most families were relatively small; only twenty-six students had three or more siblings.

IMPRESSIONS

The results of these demographic studies revealed the following:

- The incidence of work inhibition was substantial. Nearly 20 percent of the population was affected, primarily boys.

- Work inhibition appeared unrelated to academic weaknesses, since work-inhibited students existed in all groups and across the spectrum of students' academic abilities and skills.
- Work inhibition did not appear to be a function of socioeconomic class.
- Work inhibition was not related to birth order.
- The overwhelming majority of work-inhibited students were not highly disruptive to the instructional process.

Appendix B:
Information from
Parents and Educators

During the 1984–85 school year, the Curriculum Council of the Falls Church City (Virginia) Public Schools determined that the school system should develop courses of action to help work-inhibited students. To assist in this process, an article was printed in *The Focus,* a local publication, announcing formation of such a committee and inviting interested persons to become members. Thirty-nine individuals joined the committee—twenty-two parents and seventeen educators. The educators were teachers and counselors who provided services to children in grades one through twelve.

From May 1985 to May 1986, the committee met seven times. During its first meeting, the committee agreed that the problem to be considered would be "students who do not complete assigned work."

A major function of the committee was to identify the characteristics observed in these work-inhibited students. The committee was divided into small groups that included both educators and parents to discuss behaviors typical of the students being considered. Each small group recorded the descriptions and the full committee pooled the lists. The full committee then developed a list of characteristics of work-inhibited students. Parents and educators gave similar descriptions of behaviors manifested by work-inhibited students in school and home. The list of characteristics included only those descriptions that the committee agreed were generally or frequently true of work-inhibited students. The characteristics described by this committee (with additions and revisions) are included at the end of Chapter 3.

Appendix C:
A Comparative Study of Work-Inhibited and Achieving Students Measuring Self-Esteem, Attitudes Toward School, and Locus of Control

The purpose of this February 1982 study was to examine self-esteem, attitudes toward school, and locus of control in work-inhibited students in the Falls Church (Virginia) school system. In order to do this, a paired group study was conducted. Two groups were selected, each consisting of twenty-four students enrolled in grades six through ten. The experimental, or work-inhibited, group included work-inhibited students, all with extended histories of failure to complete school assignments. The control, or achieving, group consisted of students with verified long-term histories of completing school assignments in a manner at least typical of students in their respective grades.

The two groups were matched according to several criteria. They were paired according to grade enrolled in school, sex, SRA intellectual ability score, and SRA reading score. For example, a male sixth-grade, work-inhibited student who possessed average intelligence and reading skills was paired with a sixth-grade boy with similar abilities and reading skills who was *not* work-inhibited.

In addition, members of both groups all met the following criteria:

- average or above-average academic ability (4th stanine or above)
- average total reading on the SRA Achievement Series (4th stanine or above)
- enrolled in Falls Church schools for at least two years
- a mother who graduated from high school
- English-speaking
- experienced no known traumatic events within the previous two years
- no other known substantive academic, cognitive, or emotional problems

Locus of control refers to the extent to which an individual believes that what happens to him is a result of his own efforts. People who generally believe that what happens is a result of their own efforts are said to have an *inner* locus of control. Those who believe that occurrences result from forces outside their own efforts and abilities are said to have an *external* locus of control.

Attitudes toward school in this study refer to a student's belief that what happens in school is either positive or negative.

Administered to each of the two groups were three tests, including The Self-Appraisal Inventory/Intermediate Level (self-concepts), The School Sentiment Index/Secondary Level (attitudes toward school), and the Individual Achievement Responsibility Questionnaire (locus of control).

The Self-Appraisal Inventory, published by Instructional Objectives Exchange (IOX), is designed for group research and requires subjects to respond "true" or "untrue" to its seventy-seven items. Four subscales are used to measure self-concept as it relates to family, peers, school, and general outlook. A total self-concept score is provided.

The School Sentiment Index is also published by IOX. This self-report device attempts to secure, in a straightforward fashion, students' attitudes toward school. The student responds to eighty-two statements by indicating strong agreement, agreement, disagreement, or strong disagreement. Examples of the statements are: "My teacher gives assignments which are too difficult," "My teachers allow some choice in what I study in class," "Students here aren't friendly," and "Each morning I look forward to coming to school."

The Individual Achievement Responsibility Questionnaire is composed of thirty-four items; each describes either a positive or a negative achievement experience that routinely occurs in students' daily lives. Each item is followed by two alternatives, one stating that the event was caused by the child and the other stating that the event occurred because of the behavior of someone else.

The three tests were administered in one session to both the experimental and control groups. It was hypothesized that achieving students, when compared with work-inhibited students, would receive scores indicating an attribution of inner (rather than external) locus of control, a more positive attitude toward school, and higher self-esteem.

Mean scores for each of the tests were obtained, and a t test for paired groups was applied to the data. On the Individual Achievement Responsibility test, the work-inhibited group received a mean score of 23.83 and the achieving group received a mean score of 23.37. Using a one- or two-tailed test, no statistical significance was found between these two scores.

On the measure of attitude toward school (School Sentiment Index), the mean for the work-inhibited group was 201.6, com-

TABLE 4.   Self-Concept Scores, Work-Inhibited
and Achieving Group

Scale	Experimental	Control	One-tailed t test
General	13.5	14.2	P < .05
Peers	12.1	14.0	P < .01
Family	11.6	14.0	P < .001
School	10.8	13.4	P < .001
TOTAL	48.0	55.6	P < .001

pared to 218.2 for the achieving group. The achieving group score was significantly higher than that of the work-inhibited group (one-tailed test P < .001).

On the measure of self-concept (Self-Appraisal Inventory), all mean scores were significantly higher for the achieving students. The achieving group scored higher on all four sub-tests. The greatest difference was in the scores concerning school and family. A summary of the scores appears in Table 4.

The School Sentiment Index scores clearly indicate that work-inhibited students have a more negative attitude toward school than other students. Work-inhibited students are more likely to think that teachers are not interested in them or do not want to be helpful. They are more likely to believe that learning activities are boring or irrelevant. Some feel that if they had a choice, they might not go to school at all.

The significantly lower scores received on The School Sentiment Index by the work-inhibited students do not mean that students in either group were all positive or all negative in their perceptions about school life. It means only that those students who have substantial problems in completing their work feel more negative about school life than others.

In terms of locus of control, no significant differences were found between the two groups. It has been hypothesized that persons with high achievement motivation usually attribute their successes and failures to their own efforts or lack of efforts, whereas persons with low achievement motivation are more likely to ascribe their successes or lack of them to perceptions of external factors, such as, "That was easy," "I was lucky," or "The teacher gave me a break." These cognitive processes do not appear to relate to the problem of work inhibition.

While locus of control is not a determinant for poor school effort, low self-esteem is clearly related to work inhibition. Self-esteem cannot be seen, since it has to do with thoughts or "self-talk": "My Dad likes me and the way I help him in the garage." "If I do my English, I'll probably get an A." "I like Christine. She's really great and she likes me." "I wanna play football, but what if I go out and sit on the bench. Everyone will say, 'What a jerk!' Why bother?"

Few, if any, individuals have confident, positive, and realistic thoughts about all aspects of their lives. A person may have a high self-opinion about schoolwork, family, and friends, but still believe strongly that he or she could never be comfortable as a public speaker, a good athlete, or feel secure in certain social situations. Thoughts about oneself are not necessarily global; this may be observed in the scores illustrated in Table 4.

On the Self-Appraisal Inventory, scores for self-esteem were significantly lower for the work-inhibited group on all scales. It is interesting, however, that the differences between the two groups were small on the general scale. This dimension measures a more global, general estimate of self-esteem, such as "I am a cheerful person," or "I can be trusted." The implications are that work-inhibited students' perceptions of self are not necessarily negative or unworthy. Rather, their self-appraisals vary.

Negative thoughts related most significantly toward school,

e.g., "I often get discouraged in school," and thoughts about family, e.g., "I cause trouble for my family" and "I get upset easily at home."

In this sample, the students came from homes of well-educated parents who were likely to place high value on education. To fail at those endeavors most valued by parents takes a greater emotional toll on a child than to do poorly at a task that is not so critical. It is possible that poor achievement contributes to a lower perceived sense of worth by parents. Work-inhibited students are not confident about their relations with peers; however, they feel they receive even less approval from their parents.

The scores definitely support the hypothesis that, in comparison to students who complete their schoolwork, work-inhibited students have poor self-concepts and negative attitudes toward school. The scores also suggest a link between family relationships and school success.

Appendix D:
A Comparative Personality Study of Work-Inhibited and High-Achieving Students

This study, conducted in June 1985 using the High School Personality Questionnaire, compared personality traits of work-inhibited students with those of achieving students. The subjects for this study were forty-two work-inhibited students enrolled in grades six through ten (thirty-three boys and nine girls) and twenty-two achieving students enrolled in grades six through nine (twenty boys and two girls). Members of the achieving group all were successful students who maintained at least a B average.

Estimates of academic ability and achievement were obtained for all students using the Science Research Associates tests. The composite score (total score for reading, math, and language arts) was used as an indicator of academic knowledge and skills.

The mean composite normal curve equivalent (NCE) score was 60.6 for the work-inhibited group and 75.8 for the achieving group. Achievement skills for the achieving group were significantly higher than for the work-inhibited group (two-tailed t test $P < .0001$). The ability for the two groups was determined by using the Educational Ability Test. The mean NCE ability score was 63.7 for the work-inhibited group and

83.6 for the achieving group. The academic ability of the achieving group was higher (two-tailed t test P < .002).

The age of each student studied was obtained and expressed in months. The mean age was 169.7 months for the work-inhibited group and 163.3 for the achieving group. The difference in age was not significant (two-tailed t test P > .05).

There was no attempt to match the two groups according to academic abilities and skills, but both groups generally tested average to highly superior. The work-inhibited group included two students who were receiving special services for learning disabilities. Both of these students had low-average to below-average academic skills and abilities. All other members of the work-inhibited group had average to above average-skills and abilities. By almost all standards, the achieving group members were "good" students, with excellent abilities, skills, and grades.

The Jr.-Sr. High School Personality Questionnaire was administered to all sixty-four subjects. The test is designed for an age range of twelve to eighteen years. Form A of the 1968–69 edition was used. The questionnaire comprises 142 questions that require students to give an "a," "b," or "c" response. (An example: "Have you enjoyed being in drama, such as school plays?" a. yes; b. uncertain; c. no.)

Raymond B. Cattell and Mary D. L. Cattell are the authors of this well-known test published by the Institute for Personality and Ability Testing Inc. This instrument was chosen because of its breadth—fourteen dimensions of personality are measured. Descriptions of each of the dimensions are noted and mean scores are plotted in Figure 1. The solid line represents work-inhibited students and the broken line represents achieving students.

Raw scores for the High School Personality Questionnaire were converted to a Standard Ten Score referred to as a sten. These derived scores ranged from one to ten and had a mean of 5.5. The mean scores for both groups are given in Figure 1, along with the two-tailed probability t test.

The differences in scores on ten of the fourteen factors obtained from the two groups were not statistically significant. Of the twenty-eight mean scores, twenty-four fell in the average range.

The results indicated that most personality variables common to work-inhibited students are not different from those of achieving students, with some exceptions.

The greatest difference in scores occurred in Factor G, which measures persistence, drive, and a sense of duty. High scores on Factor G in typical high school groups consistently correlate positively and significantly with academic achievement. Work-inhibited students were significantly more expedient and less conforming than the achieving students.

Factor O shows another difference between the two groups. The work-inhibited group felt significantly more guilt and were more apprehensive than achieving students. In this case, the low scores obtained by the achieving students relate to self-confidence, to being less fearful, more resilient, and not as easily affected by the approval or disapproval of others.

A third significant difference was found with Factor Q3. The 4.5 sten score for the work-inhibited group fell at the lower end of the average range. The work-inhibited students showed less self-discipline than achieving students. Those who score high on this subject are able to control their emotional feelings, thus enabling them to reach their goals. High scores relate very well to academic success.

Finally, work-inhibited students were significantly more sensitive to threat and more shy than achieving students.

This comparative study showed that, for the most part, the work-inhibited population was not unique—the scores closely paralleled those of the achieving group. On Factor B, which measures abstract thinking skills, work-inhibited students scored nearly as well as the achieving group.

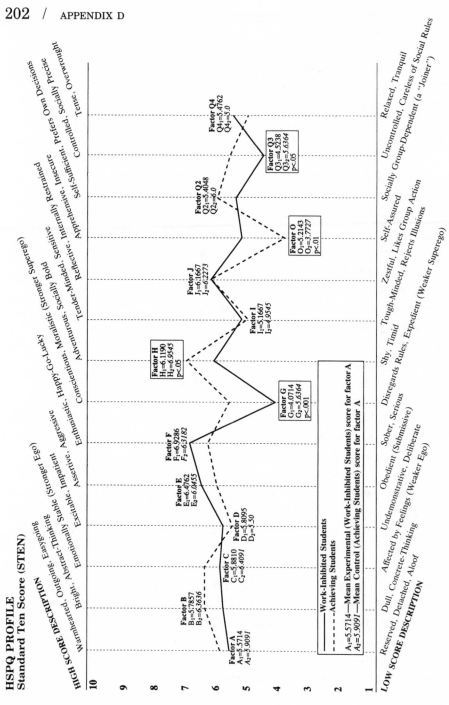

High School Personality Questionnaire: Category Descriptions, STEN scores, and STEN scores charted. Significant differences (of at least p<.05) exist between experimental and control groups' mean scores for factors G, H, O, and Q_3 (boxed on graph).

The work-inhibited population may not be characterized in broad terms as having profound emotional problems. However, these students are more likely to have difficulty in subscribing to instructional rules and to be less persistent in completing assigned tasks. Work-inhibited students also appear to experience some guilt about their shortcomings. This is encouraging since low superego strength with little guilt is associated with delinquent behavior. Work-inhibited students may have trouble following the rules of school and home, but they worry about it nevertheless.

Appendix E:
Parent and Teacher
Interviews

In January 1985, parents of fifteen work-inhibited students were interviewed to study why children become work-inhibited. The children of these parents ranged in grade placement from first through eleventh grade, and included three first-graders, one second-, one fifth-, two seventh-, six eighth-, one ninth-, and one eleventh-grader.

Each interview took approximately one hour. Eight interviews were conducted by Elizabeth M. Austin, Ed.D., together with the author, and seven interviews were conducted solely by the author.

While specific questions were asked of all parents, these discussions were also open-ended, enabling parents to describe relationships with their children, as well as the behavior and development from birth of their children.

The questions asked included:

1. How do you see the problem your child is having at school, and when did these problems begin?
2. How would you describe your child's personality?
3. Other than the completion of school tasks, what other concerns do you have about your child at home and at school?
4. What is it like to be the parent of _____?

5. Describe the circumstances of the pregnancy.

6. Describe the labor and delivery.

7. What kind of infant was _____? (Activity level, mood, distractibility, persistence, openness to new situations, etc.)

8. Method and duration of feeding?
   Pacifier or thumb sucker?
   Any bedtime problems?
   Security object?
   Toilet training—when and how, what was the child's reaction? Other major caretakers? How much of the time?

9. Describe the child's early play. (Alone, with others, what did he/she like to do?) Television viewing habits in early years?

10. Describe the child's first experiences with separation from you. (Baby-sitters, going to friends, relatives, pre-school, kindergarten.)

11. Any traumas, deaths, or extreme changes in the child's life?

12. Generally, how has school been for _____ ? Describe the relationships he/she has had with his/her teachers.

13. What does _____ like to do at home?
    What are his/her favorite activities?
    Television viewing habits now?

14. Does _____ have friends? How many? How often does he/she play with them? How would you describe his/her relationships with friends?

15. Describe _____ 's relationships with immediate family members.

16. What is your general approach to discipline? What kinds of things is _____ disciplined for? How do you feel when _____ is disciplined?

17. How have you dealt with this problem of getting work done?

18. Is there anything else you would like for us to know about _____ or your family that could be useful?

All parents spoke easily about their children and their relationships with them. All parents seemed to enjoy and have a positive regard for the children they were discussing. At the same time, they expressed distress about the problems associated with their children's poor schoolwork. This was especially true for parents of older children. These parents also stated that they were very diligent in checking up on and supervising their children. They said they found it difficult not to quiz their children every day about what work had been assigned and what needed to be accomplished.

By and large, parents reported that the children enjoyed positive early childhood experiences. Notable exceptions were two children who experienced the traumatic loss of a parent in the preschool years.

A powerful theme was one of helplessness, since the parents did not know what to do and believed the schools were similarly unable to help their children become effective students. Parents did not blame the school—they recognized that the problem was with the children. After all, some noted, no one can make you learn.

Information from Interviews with Parents of Fifteen Work-Inhibited Students

A. Number of children observed to have characteristics of work inhibition by time of onset:
   1. Prior to entrance into kindergarten: 6
   2. First or second grade: 4

3. Apparent by fourth grade: 3
4. Emerged after elementary school: 2

B. Parents reported children were generally on schedule in meeting major developmental milestones.

C. Parents believed their children's greatest problem centered on issues of work—especially schoolwork.

D. All parents believed their children's self-esteem was weak.

E. Parents of thirteen of the children tended to be "overly involved" or enmeshed in helping and directing their children.

F. Parents of two children reported that their children were psychologically (to some degree) or actually abandoned by a primary caregiver during early years.

G. Parents reported there was some estrangement in their relationships with their work-inhibited children, usually over the issue of work or performance.

H. Parents of older children said they "tried everything" to get their children to do their work.

I. None of the parents believed the school caused their children to be work-inhibited; educators just "made the problem of work inhibition worse."

J. Parents largely felt alone in coping with their children's problem.

K. Parents believed that none of the following factors caused their children to be work-inhibited:
   1. Cognitive weaknesses
   2. Teaching style
   3. Serious emotional disturbance
   4. Fine motor weaknesses
   5. Parental neglect
   6. Age at entrance into school

Eight teachers of kindergarten and first-grade students also were interviewed. They were asked if they could predict which students were at risk for work inhibition as fourth-grade students.

The response from these teachers was unanimous. They reported that in every class there are students who are at risk for work inhibition—students who need assistance and support to complete work. These students often seem to be in their own world during work time; they daydream, play with some object, or watch and talk to classmates.

Parents and teachers agree that certain children begin school lacking the self-sufficiency necessary to be academically successful. These children generally appear to have no other severe problems, and have parents who love and care for them.

Appendix F:
The Relationships Among Completion of School Assignments, Academic Skills, and Grades

Students who have difficulty completing school assignments may nevertheless acquire average to superior academic knowledge and skills as measured by achievement tests. Indeed, work-inhibited students included in the February–March 1985 survey described in Appendix A possessed academic abilities and skills comparable to those of students in the general population. This suggests that the noncompletion of school assignments is independent of the level of students' academic skills.

In May 1982, the author conducted a study to test two hypotheses. The first was that work inhibition existed among students who had good academic skills; the second was that the submission of completed academic assignments was a major determinant of report card grades.

Information was collected on all sixty-four eighth-graders at George Mason Middle School, Falls Church, Virginia. Teachers of English, social studies, science, and mathematics provided the total number of assignments given their students for the third quarter of the 1981–82 school year and, for each student, listed the number of assignments completed. The teachers also furnished each student's third-quarter grades in English, social studies, science, and math. The students' Science Research Associates (SRA) composite test scores were obtained as well; in this study, the composite scores represented academic achievement.

For each student, the ratio of assignments completed to those assigned was converted into percentages, as were the third-quarter grades earned in the four subject areas. The SRA normal curve equivalent scores also were obtained for the students, which represented their academic knowledge. The combined score represented measured skills and knowledge in reading, mathematics, and language arts.

The purpose of this study was to discover the relationships, or correlations, between and among (1) submitting completed assignments and the grades obtained; (2) submitting assignments and students' academic knowledge as represented by SRA scores; and (3) end-of-quarter grades and the SRA composite score.

Pearson correlation coefficients were .61 between ratio of assignments completed and grades, .38 between ratio of assignments completed and SRA composite score, and .40 between grades and SRA composite score. In this study, the three correlations were all significant (P < .001). It is strikingly evident, however, that the correlation (relationship) between grades and work completion was substantively higher than either of the other two correlations. As for the two lower relationships, the correlation between academic skills and assignments completed and submitted was nearly identical to the correlation between grades and academic skills and knowledge as represented by the SRA scores. One may infer from these findings that since the relationship between submitting assignments and grades is high, teachers place considerable —if not paramount—importance on the completion of work as a determinant of grades.

Furthermore, since the correlation between completion of

assignments and the SRA composite score was relatively low, it is apparent that failure to complete school assignments occurs across the spectrum of students' achievement levels, abilities, and skills. Students who possess above-average academic knowledge clearly are *not* immune from being work-inhibited.

Appendix G:
New Horizons:
A Resource Program for
Work-Inhibited Students

During the first semester of the 1986–87 school year, twenty seventh- and eighth-grade Falls Church, Virginia, students attending George Mason Middle School were enrolled in an experimental, alternative education program called New Horizons. This program was designed to provide help for work-inhibited students.

New Horizons was a one-semester course. Students met daily with their counselor/teacher and approximately six other students, and class time was used to help each student complete class and homework assignments. Counseling and instruction were provided to the group and to individuals during the class period. Students were taught a variety of skills, including techniques for effective communication with peers and adults, how to become better organized, and how to utilize their individual strengths to learn to complete assignments. The process of interaction between the counselor and each student was designed to promote more independence and improved self-esteem. It was the intent of the counselor to communicate acceptance of each individual and expectations of positive outcomes.

EVALUATION TO DETERMINE PROGRAM EFFECTIVENESS

The initial evaluation was composed of three parts. These included comparison of grades obtained before and during the first semester of the New Horizons program. Quarterly academic grades were used, including English, social studies, mathematics, science, and foreign languages. Of the twenty participating students, eleven produced an improved grade point average of .5 or above, and one student experienced a grade point average lowered by more than .5.

A student questionnaire was completed by sixteen of the New Horizons students in April 1987. The students overwhelmingly indicated that the New Horizons program was useful in helping them complete their homework. Furthermore, the students believed the program would be helpful to other students. Students' opinions differed on whether or not the program was useful in improving self-understanding, ironing out problems with teachers, and teaching how to become more effective in completing school assignments. In general, however, the results of the survey support positive attitudes toward the program by these students.

Also during April 1987, fourteen parents of the twenty students responded to a parent questionnaire. In general, the parents considered the New Horizons program useful. Ten parents agreed that the program helped their children become more effective in completing school assignments. Ten parents also reported that New Horizons helped their children develop more positive attitudes toward school. All but two parents overwhelmingly recommended continuing the program.

These early results were promising. Since the first semester of 1987–88, an additional fifty-eight George Mason Middle School students have been served in New Horizons. Current information suggests that the program was especially effective when the students received the daily help of their counselor/teacher. While long-term behaviors of work-inhibited students are not easy to change, the New Horizons program has been proven helpful.

Notes

CHAPTER 1

Underachievement is traditionally measured in relation to some standard or predicted performance. The predictors are frequently intelligence or aptitude tests against a measure of achievement.

Thorndike, R. L. (1963). *The Concepts of Over and Underachievement*. New York: Teachers College Press, Columbia University.

In 1965 Milton Kornrich surveyed the literature and found many definitions of underachievement based upon actual and predicted performance using various psychometric assessment techniques. He found no agreement among researchers as to who was and who was not an underachiever.

Kornrich, M. (1965). "A Note on the Definition of Underachievement." In M. Kornrich (ed.), *Underachievement* (pp. 459–63). Springfield, Ill.: Charles C. Thomas.

A more recent review of the research on underachievement similarly found many definitions of underachievement.

Dowdall, C., and Colangelo, N. (1982). "Underachieving Gifted Students: Review and Implications." *Gifted Child Quarterly*, 26 (4): 179–84.

A search of the literature found no studies that specified the incompletion of assignments as the definition of underachievement.

CHAPTER 3

Throughout studies on underachievers, self-concept is inextricably linked to both the characteristics and etiology of underachievement.

218 / NOTES

This link is found in studies conducted within the predominant culture as well as among minority groups.

Coopersmith, S. (1970). *The Antecedents of Self-Esteem*. San Francisco: W. H. Freeman and Co.

Fink, M. B. (1965). "Self-concept as It Relates to Academic Underachievement." In M. Kornrich (ed.), *Underachievement* (pp. 73–86). Springfield, Ill.: Charles C. Thomas.

Purkey, W. W. (1970). *Self-Concept and School Achievement*. Englewood Cliffs, N.J.: Prentice-Hall.

Wilson, J., and Black, A. (1979). "Native American Indians and Variables That Are Interrelated with Academic Achievement" (from ERIC, 1979 Abstract No. 165964).

The relationship between passive aggression and poor school performance is quite clear.

Berres, M., and Long, N. (1979). "The Passive-Aggressive Child." *The Pointer* 23 (4): 27–31.

Bricklin, B., and Bricklin, P. (1967). *Bright Child, Poor Grades*. New York: Delacorte Press.

Morrison, E. (1969). "Underachievement Among Preadolescent Boys Compared in Relation to Passive Aggression." *Journal of Educational Psychology* 60 (3): 168–73.

Students who have poor independent work habits are often described as clinging to adults, having difficulty making independent decisions, demanding attention, requiring constant direction, relying upon others, and distrusting their own abilities. Such descriptions were given by the committee studying work-inhibited students. See Appendix B. Other references include:

Dweck, C. S., and Reppucci, N. (1973). "Learned Helplessness and Reinforcement Responsibility in Children." *Journal of Personality and Social Psychology* 25 (1): 109–16.

Kohn, M. (1977). *Social Competence, Symptoms and Underachievement in Childhood: A Longitudinal Perspective*. Washington, D.C.: V. H. Winston & Sons.

McBride, C., and McFarland, M. (1987). "Children and Dependency." In A. Thomas and J. Grimes (eds.), *Children's Needs: Psy-*

chological Perspectives (pp. 151–56). Washington, D.C.: National Association of School Psychologists.

CHAPTER 4

A major contributor to the content of this chapter was child psychologist Elizabeth M. Austin, Ed.D. From April 1985 through September 1987, Dr. Austin conferred with the author on a regular basis regarding her studies of preschool and school-age children who are unmotivated to engage in the learning activities presented in preschools and primary schools.

Dr. Austin postulates that a major reason children have difficulty engaging in schoolwork is that a breakdown has occurred in the process of separation from parents and growth toward individuation. Her insights stem from her twenty years of work with preschool children as both an educator and therapist. Her theoretical constructs are based upon psychologist Margaret Mahler's theory of separation/individuation.

Austin, E. (1984). *Motivation: A Key Component to Learning.* Unpublished address, New England Kindergarten Conference, Boston.

In "He Can but He Won't," Newman, Dember, and Krug make a convincing case that the origins of work inhibition occur during infancy and are a product of the parent-child relationship. In each of the fifteen cases they studied, the child was unable to develop a positive sense of autonomy.

Newman, J., Dember, C., and Krug, O. (1973). " 'He Can but He Won't,' a Psychodynamic Study of So-called 'Gifted Underachievers.' " *The Psychoanalytic Study of the Child* 28: 83–129.

Burton R. White and his associates began in 1965 with the Harvard Preschool Project to study the development of competence in children. Their studies focused on observing how the environments of highly competent and less competent children differed. In this regard, parents were observed with their children in naturalistic environments. Using the information obtained, the Harvard Preschool Project defined parenting behaviors that facilitated childhood growth to intellectual and social competence. The project also defined parenting behaviors that inhibit such growth.

White, B., and Watts, J. (1973). *Experience and Environment: Major Influences on the Development of the Young Child.* Englewood Cliffs, N.J.: Prentice-Hall.

Other studies also link parent-child relationships to both achieving and underachieving behaviors. Studies support the theory that children prosper in an environment of clear-cut expectations while allowed to be independent.

Drews, E. M., and Teahan, J. E. (1957). "Parental Attitudes and Academic Achievement." *Journal of Clinical Psychology* 13: 328–32.

Parents of high-achieving boys were found to be more supportive, approving, trusting, and affectionate than were parents of underachieving boys.

Morrow, W. R., and Wilson, R. C. (1965). "Family Relations of Bright High-Achieving and Under-Achieving High School Boys." In M. Kornrich (ed.), *Underachievement* (pp. 188–99). Springfield, Ill.: Charles C. Thomas.

Fathers of male underachievers consistently were found to be more possessive, competitive, and nonapproving than fathers of high-achieving boys and young men.

Howe, J. J. (1980). "Underachievement in College Men." *Dissertation Abstracts International* 44: 3181 (University Microfilms No. AD681-03601).

Sunderland, B. K. (1952). "The Sentence-Completion Technique in a Study of Scholastic Underachievement." In M. Kornrich (ed.), *Underachievement* (pp. 364–75). Springfield, Ill.: Charles C. Thomas.

Teahan, J. E. (1965). "Parental Attitudes and College Success." In M. Kornrich (ed.), *Underachievement* (pp. 390–99). Springfield, Ill.: Charles C. Thomas.

High achievers report that their parents have faith in them and encourage them. By contrast, underachievers feel their parents' lack of praise and support and their own lack of independence.

Pirozzo, R. (1982). "Gifted Underachievers." *Roeper Review* 4: 18–21.

In study after study, the behavior of underachieving children has been linked to family relationships and parenting. Negative parenting includes sending mixed messages to children. Parents who agree on major issues such as setting limits tend to have more stable home environments, which promote children's growth toward security and self-confidence.

Fine, B. (1976). *Underachievers: How They Can Be Helped.* New York: E. P. Dutton and Co.

Permissive parents may overempower their children. These children are often described as demanding, spoiled, and immature. They possess weak self-esteem and have difficulty becoming independent and completing assignments.

Sherman, Z. S. (1979). "The Antiachiever: Rebel Without a Future." *The School Counselor* 2: 24–88.

CHAPTER 5

For more than ten years, James Chalfont and Margaret Pysh have gathered information regarding the problems teachers face in helping their students. In schools across America, Chalfont and Pysh have found that teachers overwhelmingly report that their primary concern is students' work habits. Specifically, teachers have been most concerned about students not completing work on time, not working independently, not making an effort to do work, and not following directions.

Chalfont, J., and Pysh, M. V. (1989). "Teacher Assistance Team: Five Descriptive Studies on Ninety-six Teams." *Remedial and Special Education* 10: 49–58.

A major thesis of this book is that work inhibition is not caused by weak academic skills or by learning disabilities. Both the National Joint Committee on Learning Disabilities and the Delegate Assembly of the National Association of School Psychologists support this point.

These two groups agree that underachievement is not synonymous with learning disabilities.

National Association of School Psychologists (1988). Editorial. *Communiqué*, June: 9.

An excellent source of information about attention-deficit disorders was published by the Virginia Department of Education:

Virginia Department of Education (1990). *Task Force Report: Attention Deficit Hyperactivity Disorder in the Schools.* Richmond, Virginia.

Information regarding causative physical/neurological factors for poor penmanship and treatment for such disorders was obtained in a June 1990 interview with Aurora Stelz, O.T.D, of Falls Church, Virginia.

CHAPTER 6

The recommendations in this chapter were developed in accordance with what have been found to be characteristics and causes of work inhibition. While recommendations have not been borrowed strictly from other sources, the following references were consulted to confirm appropriate practices.

Allen, V. L., and Feldman, R. S. (1973). "Learning Through Tutoring: Low-Achieving Children as Tutors." *Journal of Experimental Education* 42 (1): 1–5.

Amidon, E., and Flanders, N. (1967). *The Role of the Teacher in the Classroom: A Manual for Understanding and Improving Teacher Classroom Behavior—Revised Edition.* Minneapolis: Association for Productive Teaching, Inc.

Austin, E. (1984). *Motivation: A Key Component to Learning.* Unpublished address, New England Kindergarten Conference, Boston.

Dreikurs, R., and Soltz, V. (1964). *Children: The New Challenge.* New York: Hawthorn.

Glasser, W. (1969). *Schools Without Failure.* New York: Wyden.

Green, L. (1986). *Kids Who Underachieve.* New York: Simon and Schuster.

Hunter, M. (1978). *A Clinical Theory of Instruction.* Paper from the University Elementary School. Los Angeles: University of California.

Rogers, C. (1965). "A Theory of Therapy, Personality and Interpersonal Relationships, as Developed in the Client-Centered Framework." In G. Lindsey and C. Hall (eds.), *Theories of Personality: Primary Sources and Research* (pp. 469–77). New York: John Wiley and Sons.

Whitmore, J. R. (1978). "Characteristics and Causes of Underachievement in Young Gifted Children." *Roeper Review* 12 (3): 1–6.

——— (1980). *Giftedness, Conflict and Underachievement.* Boston: Allyn & Bacon.

CHAPTER 7

Recommendations were offered in Chapter 6 for educators to help work-inhibited students by means of expressions of affection and acceptance and through attentive listening. Recommendations are provided for parents to foster positive family relationships that stress the importance of affection, acceptance, and listening. In this regard, some of the same sources (Austin, Driekurs, Grier, and Rogers) were consulted. In addition, other sources were reviewed to validate recommendations to parents regarding such issues as play, discipline, household chores, and homework.

Burzynski, P. (1987). "Children and Play." In P. Thomas and J. Grimes (eds.), *Children's Needs: Psychological Perspectives* (pp. 427–34). Washington, D.C.: National Association of School Psychologists.

Drews, E. M., and Teahan, J. E. (1957). "Parental Attitudes and Academic Achievement." *Journal of Clinical Psychology* 13: 328–32.

Fine, B. (1976). *Underachievers: How They Can Be Helped.* New York: E. P. Dutton and Co.

Hester, J. (1987). "Children and Household Chores." In P. Thomas and J. Grimes (eds.), *Children's Needs: Psychological Perspectives* (pp. 298–305). Washington, D.C.: National Association of School Psychologists.

Morrow, W. R., and Wilson, R. C. (1965). "Family Relations of

Bright High-Achieving and Under-Achieving High School Boys." In M. Kornrich (ed.), *Underachievement* (pp. 188–99). Springfield, Ill.: Charles C. Thomas.

Newman, J., Dember, C., and Krug, O. (1973). " 'He Can but He Won't,' a Psychodynamic Study of So-called 'Gifted Underachievers.' " *The Psychoanalytic Study of the Child* 28: 83–129.

CHAPTER 8

Contributions to this chapter were made by the three mental health professional listed below. Each has extensive experience in providing counseling and consultative services for work-inhibited students, their parents, and their teachers.

Alan McFarland, Ph.D., licensed clinical psychologist

Maureen Lesher, M.A., N.C.S.P., school psychologist

John Curtin, Ph.D., licensed clinical psychologist

Index

Academic skills, 20–22
Acceptance, 127–28
Achievement tests, 7–8, 20–22, 78–79
Activity-oriented counseling, 156–59
Adventure, encouraging, 141
Affection, 124–27
Allowance, 143–44
Amends for negative behavior, making, 136
Anger, 34–38, 62, 87–89
Apologizing, 136
Assignments, grades and completion of, 73
Attention deficits, evaluation for, 79–82
Attention-seeking, 31
Attentive listening, 93–94
Attitudes toward school, study of, 34, 193–98
Autonomy, see Independence

Basic rules children must learn, 57
Behavior patterns, 22–23
Being themselves, children, 54
Birth order, 24
Blaming parents, 117, 119–20
Boys, 18, 60–63
    aggressive or assertive behavior and, 61–62
    anger and, 62
    fathers and, 58–60
    societal factors and, 62–63

Characteristics of work-inhibited students, 26–44
    attitudes toward school, 34
    dependency, 27–31
    desire for success, 39–40
    list of, 42–44
    passive aggression, see Passive aggression
    peer relationships, 38
    personality, 40–41
    perspective on, 39–40
    poor penmanship, 39
    self-esteem, 31–33
    study of, 40–41, 199–203
    summary of, 26–27
Chores, 146–48
Classroom behaviors, 75
Class size, 30–31
Clumsiness, 77
Cognitive Abilities Test, 7
Company of younger children, 31
Competitiveness, 106, 130
Conferences:
    parent-teacher, 153
    student-teacher, 102
Confidence, 49
Confident expectations, 102, 112–13
Cooperation among students, 106
Counseling, see Guidance counselors; Psychotherapists; School counselors

Decision-making, 115
Defining the problem, 3–16
    case study, 9–16
    underachievement, 6–8
    work inhibition, 8–9
Demanding children, 55–56
Demographic studies, 181–90
Department of Education, U.S., 149
Dependency, 27–31, 124
    class size and, 30–31
    difficulty of work and, 30
    proximity of teacher and, 27
    see also Independence
Diagnosis of work inhibition, see Identification and evaluation of work inhibition
Discipline, see Negative behavior, parental limits on
Disruptive behavior, 22–23

Early determinants of work inhibition, 45–65

making amends, 136
no, being able to say, 133–34
removing privileges, 136
rules, 132–33
separating child from the scene, 135
spanking, 136–37
threats, 136–37
Negative feedback, 110
No, being able to say, 133–34
Nonjudgmental listening, 93–94
Noticing student outside classroom, 92–93
Nurturing relationship, building teacher-student, 91–98

Observation, attention deficit diagnosed by, 81
Occupational therapists, 82–83
Otis-Lennon Test of Mental Abilities, 19
Overempowered children, 55–57, 134

Paraprofessionals, 107–9
Parents:
blaming, 117, 119–20
communication with teachers, 152–53
consulting with counselors, 162–65, 171
criticism by, 128
disapproval by, 57–60, 124
education of, 23
frustrations of, 4–6
help from, *see* Parents' role in helping
identification of work inhibition, 76
independence and, 51–52, 124
interviews of, 205–9
overempowering, 55–57
overprotective, 52–55
self-esteem of children and, 33
separation and divorce of, 23–24
as teachers, 144–46
worries of, 53, 55
Parents' role in helping, 123–53
acceptance, 127–28
affection, 124–27
communication with educators, 152–53
homework, 148–52
household chores, 146–48
listening, 128–29
perspective on the problem, 153
play, 129–31
positive reinforcement, 137
promoting autonomy, 138–44
setting limits on negative behaviors, 131–37
strengthening family relationships, 124–31
as teachers, 144–46
Partial responses, 37
Passive aggression, 34–38, 159–60

boys and, 62
as expression of anger, 34
forgetfulness, 34–35
partial responses, 37
response of parents or teachers to, 37
verbal lawyers, 35–36
withholding, 36–37
Peabody Individual Assessment Test, 79
Peer relationships, 38
peer support, 106
play, 131
Penmanship, 39, 77, 82–83
Persistence, 98–105
mentors, 99–103
varying assignments, 103–4
working incrementally, 104–5
Personality, 63–64
Personality tests, 86
Play, 129–31
Positive coping skills, 56–57
Positive expectations, statement of, 102, 112–13
Positive reinforcement, 104, 112–13, 137, 146, 147
Predicted performance, 6–8
Principals, identification of work inhibition by, 70–71
Privileges, removing, 136
Procrastination, 36–37
Professional resource programs, 107–9
Psychological evaluation, 83–90
Psychotherapists, 155, 172–77
attention disorder diagnosed by, 81
obstacles to therapy, 174–75
selection of therapist, 175–76
therapeutic approach, 176–77

Recess, denying, 117, 119
Recognition with responsibility, 114–15
Removing child from scene of negative behavior, 135
Repeating a grade, 117, 118
Resource programs, professional, 107–9
Responsibility, recognition with, 114–15
Retention, 117, 118
Rorschach test, 13
Rules, 57, 132–33

Safety patrols, 114
Sarcasm, 95–96
School counselors, 155–57
activity-oriented counseling, 156–59
in elementary schools, 156–65
guiding principles for, 156
for teenagers, 165–71
Schools, plan for helping for, 120–22
Schools Without Failure (Glasser), 92
Secondary-school counseling, 165–71
Self-acceptance, 160
Self-consciousness, 31

1/98"
12 5/00